£2.

FARM YOUR GARDEN

Also by Joanna Smith

VILLAGE COOKING

FARM YOUR GARDEN

Joanna Smith

SIDGWICK & JACKSON

LONDON

First published in Great Britain by
Sidgwick and Jackson Limited

Copyright © 1977 Joanna Smith

Line drawings by Eileen Browne

ISBN 0 283 98311 6

Printed in Great Britain
by Latimer Trend & Company Ltd, Plymouth
for Sidgwick and Jackson Limited
1 Tavistock Chambers, Bloomsbury Way
London WC1A 2SG

FOR

Emily, Bertie and Flora

Acknowledgements

HEARTFELT THANKS are due to John and Margaret Langley for help with poultry problems and for introducing us to the excellent British Waterfowl Association; Andy Clark for vetting the chapter on sheep; Avery Backhouse and Julian David for advice on pigs; Hazel Pope for writing about her goats and Matthew Thorpe for the chapter on the house cow; Cyril Ayley for his helpful information on fish farming; my dairy farming mother for sorting out the complexities of grass management; my husband Alan for the chapter on trees; Charles Talbot for much research into the law as it affects garden farming. The doctor who helped me with the chapter on health prefers to remain anonymous for professional reasons, but he knows how grateful I am. The book has been much enhanced by Eileen Browne's drawings and the photographs specially taken by Harold Chapman.

J.S.

Contents

List of Plates

INTRODUCTION

Farming your Garden

WE HAVE been farming our garden now for five years. Before that we gardened our garden. We mowed and clipped and weeded, but every year we were more resentful of the expense and the repetitive, endless labour. Gradually we began to fence grassy areas. A neighbour lent us some sheep to act as mowing machines. We bought some ducks, then some geese. Suddenly we found that we were away – vegetables were growing, ducks laying, geese mowing, hens clucking, sheep lambing, and we were doing something more interesting than outdoor housework. We have made many mistakes, but now we are seeing results. Our food bills are a third of their former size and as I write (late summer) we have not touched a mowing machine for four months. Farming our garden has paid off. We could sell our surplus, but prefer to freeze, preserve and bottle or give presents.

This is not to say that garden-farming is trouble-free; far from it. Animals are a great tie and impose rigorous obligations on their owners. They must be fed and watered every day and kept clean and healthy; goats and cows must be milked twice a day; fences must be attended to. In every case, I have tried to put the cons as well as the pros for keeping the animal or bird under discussion, before considering in detail how this should be done. I have also enlisted the help of a lawyer and a doctor for the two final chapters, and they go into the legal and health problems which might arise.

A garden farm will certainly keep you busy. On the other hand, anyone who has a garden is going to spend some time working in it, and work on the garden farm can to some extent replace ordinary garden work. A garden farm will have to receive regular attention and will thus curtail its owner's freedom, but how much freedom do most of us really have? Most people are firmly tied to their homes by the obligations of daily life: children have to go to school, to be met after school, to be fed; bread-winners have to catch the train to work each morning; most people's incomes cannot stretch to frequent holidays or weekends away from home. So, if your life keeps you in one place, if you enjoy animals and birds and being out of doors, consider farming your garden.

I am writing this book because I wished so much I had had such a book when we embarked on farming our garden. There are indeed books; they are written by experts on every conceivable subject, or they are written by people who have relinquished an ordinary, humdrum working life for the ideal of a return to the land. For the beginner, with very limited resources of land, money and time, who wants to have a tangible return from odd little bits of ground, who wants food scraps to be turned into eggs, slugs to be transformed into table ducklings or grass into Christmas geese, there is no book that answers his questions. The reason for this is that garden-farming has been out of fashion. We in Britain have only recently emerged from a time of fatness, when people have not been bothering to use their ground. There is a lot of hard work involved in vegetable gardening, poultry-keeping and so on, and quite naturally people stopped trying to produce their own food while the money was easy.

The books we have found useful have been those published during the 1930s and 40s; they are of course out of date in many ways, but they were written for people like ourselves. We find them in second-hand bookshops, on stalls at bazaars, in charity shops and other odd places. The rest of our knowledge has come from helpful neighbours and our own mistakes.

In five years we have not been able to explore all the possibilities of our garden. We have, however, been able to draw on the experience of friends and neighbours, many of whom have contributed to this book. The jobs that these people manage to do in addition to their garden-farming may encourage others, as it has encouraged us. Hazel Pope, who has written on keeping goats, is a full-time teacher with three school-age children. John Langley, who keeps waterfowl on a large scale and is editor of the magazine of the British Waterfowl Association (a very useful organization for anyone who keeps waterfowl, whether wild or domestic), is motoring correspondent of the *Daily Telegraph* and yet finds time to look after all his lovely birds. Matthew Thorpe, a barrister with a demanding practice in London, finds time to attend to two house cows among many other animals and also organize a most fruitful kitchen garden. Su Gooders, who greatly helped me with the bee-keeping chapter, is a full-time photographic agent. Cyril Ayley, a busy bank manager, has contributed his experience of fish farming. There are many others who have given me notes on their successes and mistakes, or who have discussed them with me at length and I should like to thank them all for bearing with my obsession so patiently and for so long. If a friend said: 'I saw a very good film last night,' I was quite likely to reply, 'That reminds me: do you know where I can get a toe punch for ducklings?'

The obsessive phase is now, happily, over. Our garden farm is now just a small part of the way we live; it takes up comparatively little of our time. We do not attempt to be self-sufficient, only to do things we enjoy while supplementing our income and saving ourselves trouble and expense. For example, although wood gathering and chopping is very hard work, it is work that we happen to like and so we have open wood fires and a Norwegian wood-burning stove to give background heat. On the other hand, there are several jobs that I do not like, such as weeding, so our vegetable gardening is confined to vegetables that are easy to grow and can fend for themselves. Nor do we have the yields of apples that we should, because I dislike spraying and pruning.

In this book I am suggesting ways in which everybody, whatever their foibles and whatever the peculiarities, potentialities or limitations of their gardens, can use their space to their own benefit in their own way.

CHAPTER ONE

Poultry

OF ALL our enterprises, the poultry give us the most pleasure and the least trouble. They provide us with really delicious eggs and meat at a very economical price. They use little space, eat our kitchen- and garden-waste and destroy pests. We find them beautiful, comical and fascinating; and the Christmas-present problem is made much easier; few people would not be pleased to receive a goose or a capon. Poultry droppings activate and enrich compost; eggshells provide lime and can also go on the compost heap. The feathers can be used for pillows and dusters. Geese are efficient lawnmowers and watch-dogs; ducks dispose of slugs; hens are excellent scarifiers and nitrogen dispensers. Children, even small children, can really help with poultry and this is a very good thing, for looking after any sort of livestock requires responsibility, method and observation – surely qualities to be encouraged.

So what are the snags of poultry keeping? They are very few. The worst is probably the cost of setting up the operation. When all is running smoothly, the only jobs are to keep the birds clean, comfortable, fed and watered, and if you have an efficient layout this should take very little time. Neighbours' objections are likely to be to noise, vermin, smell or unsightliness. Good management

A broody hen with pheasant chicks.

Tea-time for our hens, ducks and geese.

Children can help . . .

should avoid these and the diplomatic gifts of eggs should placate most people.

HENS, BANTAMS, DUCKS OR GEESE?

Hens or bantams are the best choice for a small garden. They do not need very much space; indeed, hens can be kept entirely under cover in battery cages or on deep litter. It would be better not to keep a cockerel unless you are well away from neighbours, as the crowing is constant and amazingly loud from dawn onwards. The hens will lay just as well without him. Bantams eat less than hens; their eggs are small but the yolks are comparatively large, so the eggs are quite adequate for most purposes. Bantams are beautiful and brave: a cock bantam has been known to attack a fox in defence of his wives; the hen bantams make wonderful mothers and many people keep bantams to provide foster-mothers for other fowls.

Ducks are marvellous layers and cheap to keep where the habitat suits them. They are expensive to keep in runs, for they are voracious feeders, demolishing up to 30 per cent more food than hens. If given their freedom they will forage around and find quite a high proportion of their food for themselves. The eggs are good eating but difficult to sell as they are popularly (and wrongly) supposed to be poisonous. The whites of duck eggs will not whip, so if you are addicted to meringues or soufflés you will find yourself buying hens' eggs from time to time, or keeping a few hens as well.

Geese need a lot of ground and are possible to keep only in a very large garden. They are extremely noisy and would not be suitable for anyone who has close neighbours. They will accept your own family but can terrorize visiting children or even timorous adult visitors, so you may have to fence them away from the house. They have other anti-social habits too; being very curious creatures they nibble with their powerful beaks at anything which intrigues them – such as visitors' cars. At every step they deposit large green droppings.

Whichever type of fowl you choose to keep, it is worth considering how the birds will fit into your life. If you have a full-time job or are away most of the day you should plan to have a completely fox-proof run with proper outdoor food hoppers and water drinkers from which the birds can help themselves at any time. Alternatively you might consider an indoor system. If you also keep dogs and cats you will almost certainly find that they will not attack the birds, but marauders from other gardens can be a problem and the runs may have to be roofed over with wire netting.

B

SITING THE RUNS

Wire fencing six feet high is not very pretty. When planning the run it makes sense to plant a screen of shrubs or to place it among trees – the birds will enjoy the shade. The smaller the space the neater and trimmer the poultry yard must be; there is no need for those slimy runs, rusting, sagging wire and sordid shacks, all nettles and corrugated iron.

FOOD STORAGE

Leave room beside the run for a tidy shed in which to store food and equipment. If possible have a stand-pipe beside it; this will save a great deal of time and effort and could probably also be used for watering the vegetables. If for any reason it is impossible to have piped water, have a large water butt and keep it filled up with a hose. The butt should be sluiced out frequently, so there must be a water outlet at the base, or it must be light enough to turn upside down.

Chickens

HOW MANY CHICKENS?

Twice as many laying hens as there are people in the household will provide enough eggs all the year round.

STARTING OFF

Hens start to lay at about eighteen or nineteen weeks old. Birds of this age can be bought as point-of-lay pullets; they are advertised for sale in local newspapers and farming magazines such as *Farmers Weekly*. They are expensive, but if you buy these you are spared the expense and trouble of rearing them and they have all their egg-laying life before them. Go to someone trustworthy, with a reputation to maintain.

When hens or pullets are moved they need time to adjust to their new circumstances. Pullets at point of lay will not start to lay until they have settled down, and this will take perhaps two or three weeks.

A cheaper alternative is to buy older hens, and these are likely to be ex-battery birds. They are sometimes advertised for sale but you are more likely to find them by asking around. Corn merchants, farmers, the local fishmonger or greengrocer who sells 'farm eggs' might be able to put you in touch with a battery egg-producer.

Once again the hens will need time to adjust. They will lay the eggs already in the pipeline, but after two or three days they will stop laying while they settle in. Be prepared for the dreadful appearance of these unfortunate hens when they come from the battery: they will not know how to perch; their claws, which have not been worn down by scratching, will be so long they seem to trip over them; they will have bald patches where their feathers have been worn away; their combs will be pale, their eyes lack lustre; and I maintain that their eggs will be tasteless. But a month later they will be unrecognizable.

We started off with ex-battery hens. We calculated that even if the birds were bad layers they were still a very cheap form of meat, so we bought twice as many birds as we needed. In fact they all laid very well and soon adapted to their new liberty. Many other people have had the same experience and I would recommend these hens as the best choice for the beginner.

It is possible to buy day-old chicks or feathered chicks of about seven to eight weeks old and rear them up to point of lay but, with the price of chicken food what it is, I do not think you would gain by doing so. (It is also quite probable that you would not rear such good birds as a professional would.)

BREEDS

Different birds like different soils and climates. In our area the Rhode Island Red/Light Sussex cross reigns supreme. Though dowdy in appearance, with brown feathers and yellow legs, she is a very good layer and does well on our clay. The flesh is rather yellow but it tastes as good as the white-fleshed varieties. Unless you want to breed your own birds (and this is a skill of its own), I would recommend buying high-egg-producing hybrids of a type that is available in your area.

The Maran is very popular among backyard poultry keepers; she is very lovely to look at with her tight black speckled feathers and she lays spectacular eggs, large and coffee-brown, but, alas, very few of them compared to the less glamorous laying hybrids. Marans make good table birds, however, plump and white-fleshed.

SYSTEMS

Free range

Free-range hens need really wide open spaces. Ten birds to the acre is recommended, but they will stray far more widely than this. Hens are omnivorous: they will destroy a vegetable garden in a very short time and make short work of your compost or dung heap with their powerful feet. Free-range hens are best housed away from the vegetable garden in movable arks. See page 171 for the addresses of suppliers. They lay throughout the morning, so unless you are prepared to keep them in until midday you will have to hunt for the eggs. Magpies and jackdaws will be looking out for them too. On the other hand, their eggs will be full of flavour and the yolks a good colour, they will find a considerable amount of food for themselves and they will be hardy and disease-free.

You will have to erect formidable defences around your garden to keep the hens away. On balance, I think that for most people the disadvantages of the free-range method outweigh the advantages.

Houses and runs

This is the method that we use, in common with most other backyard poultry keepers. With good management it works very well. You can either keep your hens in the house during the winter or bad weather, in which case you will have to allow 4 feet square floor space for each hen, or allow them out in all weathers. For this you must allow 100 square feet run space for each hen, but you will save on house space, litter and cleaning out. For six hens this means a house of 6 feet by 4 feet and a run of 30 feet by 20 feet (600 square feet).

Intensive methods

There are two ways of keeping hens intensively. One is to keep them in battery cages, which would have to be home-made. The other is to keep them permanently in their house on deep litter, which is dry and not at all smelly if looked after properly. Of the two, the battery method is more efficient, as hens kept indoors on deep litter become bored and develop very unpleasant behaviour, such as cannibalism. Battery birds live their lives unable to follow any of their natural instincts, to scratch, to take dust baths, to perch; surely they must be dull and deprived creatures. Nevertheless, they lay eggs in great numbers and are of course easy to look after.

HOUSING

Once you have decided on the type and size of house that your hens will need, the cheapest way to acquire one is to watch the advertisements in a local paper. New houses can be bought (a list of addresses is given on page 171) but they are expensive, of course. Almost any shed can be converted to a chicken house; handy people can make their own.

Hens like their comforts. The house should be well lit; it

Portable poultry ark for up to eighteen hens, for use on rough ground or an orchard.

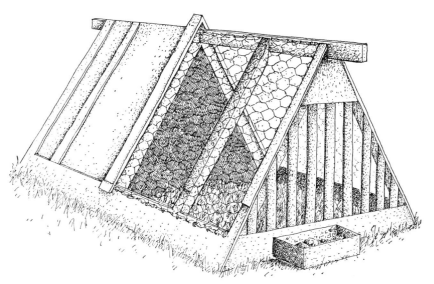

Portable fold unit for six hens, suitable for moving to and fro across your lawn.

should be airy, but ventilated at the top so that there is not a
howling gale. The laying boxes should be warm and comfortable,
off the floor; allow one box for every three hens. Perches should
be long enough for all the hens to sleep on – you should allow

Nesting-box with sloping
top to discourage roosting.

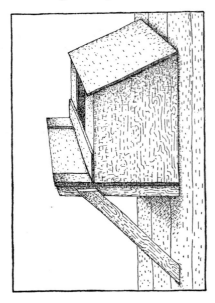

Perches and droppings board

Hen house for twelve hens

A suitable house, made of wood on brick stands, for use with an outdoor run. This will hold up to one dozen hens, with run provided, or free range, or six hens kept intensively.

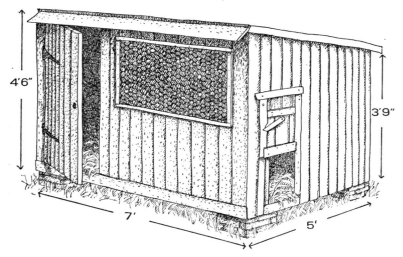

The ventilators in the back of the house are covered with wire netting, as is the window of the front of the house. If the hens are to be kept intensively, i.e., indoors all the time, the house would be too dark for them, so two extra windows should go on the sides of the house and an inner door, made of wire netting on a wooden frame, should be fitted so that the main door can be left open in all but the worst weather; this will provide fresh air and sunlight for the hens.

nine inches of perch room for each bird. The perches should be rounded at the top and not too thick – about two inches wide.

The house has to be cleaned occasionally, so a house that you can stand up in is ideal. At any rate it must be easy to reach into and clean out and high enough to accommodate the build-up of litter. The fittings must be movable too, for easy cleaning.

We converted a roofless brick shed into a chicken house, with the help of an amateur handyman and using diagrams from a wartime poultry booklet published by the *Daily Express*. It cost us roughly £25 and should last our lifetime. But we made mistakes: the pophole opened from the inside instead of the outside, and the droppings board was too narrow.

Left: **Pophole for a hen house.** *Right:* **Rack for greens,** which are best kept off the floor.

FENCING

Fencing should be of ordinary chicken wire (one inch) mesh and six feet high – hens can fly. Posts should be strong and firmly dug in; the gate should be wide enough to admit a wheelbarrow, and it helps to be able to fasten it from both sides.

Bury the wire into the ground or the chickens will stratch a way underneath it. Burying discourages foxes too.

The run must be divided into two. Use the runs alternately to give each a rest. The house could be between the two runs with a pophole on each side.

In suburban areas there may be trouble with marauding cats; if so, you will have to cover the top of the run with wire. You can sometimes buy chicken wire in garden shops, otherwise you will have to go to a major ironmonger. Ring up first; many iron-mongers do not stock it. The Country Gentlemen's Association will deliver it to members (their address is on page 170). Garden shops have posts, at a price. If you are able to cut your own, chestnut or larch wood is the best; treat with creosote before use.

RUN MANAGEMENT

Grass runs

If you want a grass run, it will have to be big because hens love eating grass and scratching up the roots; their droppings then finish the grass off completely, unless the range is big enough.

If you can allow enough space for a grass run this is much the best both for you and for the birds. Divide the run into two or three; do not let the hens eat the grass right down but keep moving them on. Lime the run they have left and run a rotary mower over it, or scythe it, to discourage any rank coarse growth. If the runs show signs of wear, which they will in a dry summer or a wet winter, keep the hens in while they recover or you will have to dig and re-seed the runs. If you do have to do this, buy a heavy use lawn mixture of grass seed, dig over the run, sow, rake in the seed and then stamp it in or roll it. If the soil is loose the hens will scratch it all up in a jiffy, and the whole effort will have been wasted.

It is best to protect the grass seed against wild birds while you are waiting for it to germinate. Cover the area with a garden net or wire netting.

In each run there must be a scratching area large enough for dust baths and here you can forget grass. Encourage the hens to use it by feeding grain and garden waste there; with any luck they will do all their scratching in this one corner.

Earth runs

Most people have small earth runs. Again, divide the run into two; rest the runs alternately every three months or so; first digging them over and liming them. The run in use can be kept pleasant to walk on (or scratch in) by using a sort of outdoor deep-litter system. Wheelbarrow in all the weeds and garden rub-bish and spread layers of dead leaves and cinders. The hens will enjoy picking all this over and they will sort through it again and

again. Scatter their grain in it; they will have endless amusement
and exercise in finding it. When changing runs, rake up the outdoor litter and put it on the compost heap.

FEEDING

The wartime books that we found so useful when we started
were all quite useless on the subject of feeding, for everything has
changed radically over the past few years. 'Chicken feed', once a
synonym for paltry sums of money, is now extremely expensive,
and alternatives to commercial layers' mash and layers' pellets are
hard to come by. The home producer should however, without
more than average success, have eggs at approximately half the
price they are in the shops.

Hens need two meals a day. The first can be grain, for speed.
(Free-range hens need nothing but grain.) We give ours one
handful each of mixed corn first thing in the morning and throw
it on the ground. Sometimes we buy a sack of wheat for a change
as it is rather cheaper, but mixed corn is better for the hens.

About an hour before sunset in winter and around 6 p.m. in
summer the hens have their main meal. Give the hens as much
food as they can clear up comfortably by roosting time. This
meal can be of layers' pellets, which are slightly more expensive
than layers' mash, but of course more convenient and less wasteful, as they are fed dry and any surplus can easily be put away for
the next day. Both pellets and mash should be fed into containers
for cleanliness and to avoid waste.

We ourselves prefer layers' mash, which can be mixed with
kitchen scraps, sour milk, and so on; with a family of five which
includes three children we have quite a lot of scraps. The mash is
mixed with water to a crumbly consistency; in winter the hens
appreciate a warm mash.

We go direct to the large local corn merchant for foodstuffs.
They will deliver, but they have a high delivery charge; it might
be worthwhile trying to find someone to share a carload of foodstuffs and spread the cost of the petrol. The pet shop also sells
layers' mash and pellets but naturally it takes a retail profit.

It is not worth trying to make up your own mashes, buying the
ingredients from the corn merchant; the ingredients are hard to
obtain and it can even work out more expensive. This is because
the handling and storage costs add enormously to what might be
expected to be cheap ingredients. It is definitely worthwhile to
try to find supplementary sources of food which can be added to
the mash, not just to save money but to add flavour to eggs and
meat.

Gleaning: Those who live in the country and are on good terms with farmers can ask permission to glean. Maize cobs are particularly popular with hens and give the egg yolks a marvellous colour.

Greengrocers: It is worth asking what happens to the wastage from the greengrocer. Greens can be hung up in string bags in the hen house or in bunches from a nail and will be greeted with enthusiasm.

Bakers: Small bakers often have stale bread or a batch of overdone loaves which one can buy.

Fishmongers: Fish is an invaluable source of protein; our fishmonger lets us have as many scraps as we wish each week in return for a dozen eggs. We boil up the scraps in a cauldron and then put them into the freezer for use throughout the week. Without the freezer we would have to collect the scraps more often. I must warn those with sensitive noses about the smell of boiling fish.

Crops from the garden: Lawn mowings can be given to the hens, but only as much as they can clear up in a day or the mowings will start to go musty. In dry weather you can spread out the mowings on a path or some other dry place and make them into a sort of minced hay. This can be stored when quite dry in bins and given to the hens when you are short of other greenstuffs. Ordinary hay can lead to crop binding (an unpleasant form of congestion in the crop), and should not be given to hens.

Hens will eat most things out of the garden (which is why they must stay in their run). They particularly appreciate parsnips, carrots, Jerusalem artichokes, turnip tops and all forms of greens. Kale is a good crop to grow for them if you have a corner to spare. Potatoes they adore, but they like them to be cooked. A row of sunflowers along the outside of the run are not only decorative; the sunflower heads can be stored and given to the hens, who relish the seeds.

WATER

Hens must have plenty of clean, fresh water available at all times. We use Albert drinkers (see page 171 for the addresses of suppliers). They are handy to carry around and keep the water clean. Of course, any container can be used for water. The containers and food troughs must be scrubbed out at least once a week in winter and twice a week in summer or they become slimy. This is why it is so convenient to have a piped water supply close to the henhouse; it really does save time.

Grit

All birds need grit; laying birds also need a source of lime. The hens must have a container full of flint or granite grit to help them chew up their food and another container of limestone grit or oystershell to help them form their eggshells. Buy grit from the feed suppliers or pet shops. To save on oystershell, dry empty eggshells thoroughly in the stove or other warm place, crush them and give them to the hens in their mash or in the grit container.

Litter

Books tell one to use straw, but its price may prove prohibitive. When the house is cleaned out, lay down straw or wood shavings, which make a nice bouncy base for the litter and take the chill off a concrete floor, if you have one. Then add sawdust and dry leaves. Don't buy the sawdust from a pet shop or corn merchant. It is much cheaper to go to a sympathetic timber yard bearing your own sacks. The bags that the chicken food came in will do, or you can pick up polythene fertilizer sacks from the ditches along any country road, or ask a farmer to give you a few.

If the henhouse is watertight and the hens do not splash water

Splash-proof water bucket for the hen house.

or mash around, the litter will keep remarkably dry. Top up with more litter as necessary and clear it out about every six months. If enough litter is used there will be no smell or mess.

HYGIENE

Buy a good aerosol insecticide for pets, such as Cooper's, from the pet shop. For economy, buy an insecticide powder as well. Put the powder into the nesting boxes, the sockets of the perches and any other cracks and crannies. When the hens have gone to roost and are quietly lined up on their perches for your convenience, go in with a torch and squirt them with the aerosol spray. Repeat after five days. Then they will have no trouble with red mite, lice or fleas.

When cleaning out the house, puff insecticide powder around the floor, creosote the woodwork and limewash the inside of the house with ordinary garden lime mixed with water.

Particularly in the winter, provide an indoor dustbath for the hens in a large box, or nail a plank on its side across one corner of the house. Fill up the bath with dry earth, or sand, cinders or sawdust, and mix in some insecticide powder.

BROODY HENS

Hens generally go broody in warm weather, any time from about April on. A broody hen becomes addicted to sitting in the nesting boxes; if anyone comes near she fluffs out her feathers and makes what I can only call a broody noise. She stops laying, has little interest in food and goes off into a dream, showing no fear of being handled.

The recipe for curing broodiness is quickly to place the hen in in an uncomfortably draughty box where she can see the others and to feed her a high-protein diet, such as an extra helping of fish or meat scraps. If she is very broody she will take two or three weeks to come back into lay, but if caught in time she will probably be laying again within a few days.

BREEDING AND REARING

Hatching

It is almost irresistible to attempt to hatch and rear chicks. The simplest and cheapest way is to let a broody hen do it for you. Make a comfortable nest out of straw in a coop. A box or barrel will do, but the hen should be kept a prisoner or she may decide to wander off and make another nest somewhere else.

As an experiment I allowed a very broody little hen to sit on some eggs in her favourite laying box in the henhouse. She sat most faithfully but after coming off the nest to feed she was perplexed to find eggs in several of the nesting boxes, and often went back to the wrong clutch. She only managed to hatch two of her eggs and if the summer had not been so exceptionally warm I think that even these two would have been chilled.

A puff of insecticide before she starts to sit is a good idea. Give her a clutch of fertile eggs; give her as many as she can cover comfortably – twelve to eighteen is about right; if you have no cockerel you can buy fertile eggs from someone who has. Eggs can be kept in a cool place for several days before being put under the hen but once she starts to sit they must be kept warm continuously or the embryo will be chilled and will die. The chicks hatch on the twenty-first day. Keep the hen confined until they are all hatched or she may lose patience.

While the hen is sitting she should be let off the nest for five minutes. She will not excrete on the nest, so it is necessary for her to do this while she is having her airing; if she is slow, lift her up and drop her to the ground; the wing-flapping should do the trick. On cold days, cover the eggs with straw while she is off the nest. Put corn, water and grit where she can reach them.

The chicks need no food at all for the first twenty-four hours. They should have water, but the container must be small or they may get wet and chilled, or even drown. I use an ice-cube tray from the refrigerator with the grid in it. Buy chick crumbs (less wasteful than mash) from your corn merchants or pet shop. Seven pounds of chick crumbs will go a long way. They should be fed three times a day – but not overfed: watch to see that the food is cleared up within fifteen minutes or so. A wire run attached to the coop made of half-inch mesh will keep the chicks safe from magpies and rats. Move the coop and run over the lawn; the short grass is very good for chicks. The mistake I made at first was to have a run that I could not open from the top for easy feeding and watering, so every time I fed the chicks they escaped.

Never put a hen with chicks or any other baby birds in a run where the babies can escape through the mesh while the hen cannot. The babies will be at the mercy of any predator. I have a friend who lost some goslings in this way. So long as the babies are with the hen she will protect them with amazing courage. I have seen a hen attack a terrier that came too near her chicks.

When the chicks become too big for the coop and run they must have a run and house (a coop will do) of their own or they will be chivvied about by the older hens. At this stage they can be fed on grain and growers' pellets. Ideally the young cockerels should be kept separately for fattening but this is not always possible.

Day-old chicks

A commercial hatchery is the best place to buy day-olds; they are already sexed and if they are not of good laying stock the hatchery would soon be out of business. For the same reason, you can be sure they are free from disease.

The snag is that many hatcheries dislike supplying chicks in small quantities and I count myself lucky to have obtained some. It may be possible to arrange with a neighbour who keeps poultry on a large scale to have a dozen chicks from one of his consignments. (The chicks cost me around £4 a dozen, 1976 prices.) The hatchery will often give you a few cockerel chicks free, if you want them, with your dozen pullets.

Rearing day-old chicks

A broody hen will rear the chicks if introduced to them with care. She must be really broody and must have been sitting on eggs for a week or so. Wait until dusk and then put in one or two chicks. If she rejects them, wait an hour and try again. Push the chicks right under her feathers. When her manner changes, put in the rest of the chicks and remove the eggs.

If she will not accept the chicks, or if you have no broody, then chicks must be reared in a brooder (see page 32).

To rear or not to rear

Rearing your own stock takes space, time, energy and money. An ex-battery hen in lay will cost no more than a day-old chick with five or six months of feeding before it starts to produce. However, those who want to do it will do it. We would hate to be without our chicks, ducklings and goslings, and faithful mother hens. It would be rash, too, to assume that it will always be cheaper to buy in stock than to rear it. When I wrote *Village Cooking* (published by Sidgwick & Jackson, 1974), concentrating on economical recipes, veal was an expensive, rich man's food and puddings were cheap and filling. No sooner had the book gone to press than the collapse in beef prices had flooded the shops with cheap veal, while the sugar shortage sent the cost of puddings soaring. Perhaps similar price fluctuations will bring back the sitting hens; I hope so.

Incubators

Unfortunately it is not always possible to find a broody hen just when she is wanted and the only answer to the problem is to use an incubator. At the moment there is no cheap, small incubator on the market; if only some enterprising manufacturer would produce one! But for suppliers of larger incubators, see page 171.

Using an incubator

It is recommended to turn on the incubator for about a week before setting the eggs, to ensure that it is running at an even temperature.

Select normal-sized eggs free from all cracks or blemishes and store them in a cool place. Turn the eggs over twice a day. It is easy to get muddled doing this and the best thing is to mark the eggs on one side, gently, with a pencilled cross. Thus all the crosses will either be uppermost, or they will all be invisible, and you will not miss an egg or turn one twice by mistake. Turning should be done morning and evening when the eggs are in store and three to four times a day when they are in the incubators.

A sitting hen's body provides the necessary moisture for naturally reared eggs; those in an incubator require moisture, and the necessary instructions will come with the machine.

Rearing

Once the chicks are hatched they can be put into a brooder, which can be home-made. You can use a cardboard grocery box with a sixty-watt bulb suspended about nine inches from the floor. Net the top of the box to allow ventilation and to stop the chicks jumping out (they are very mobile). After ten days they can be moved to a larger pen with an infra-red heater. Small numbers of chicks can be reared in a warm kitchen or even the greenhouse. After a further two weeks they can be put out in a wire run in warm weather and brought back to the warmth at night, or if the weather turns cold. Harden them off gradually until they no longer require heat but merely shelter, at five to six weeks. The main thing is that, if using reliable equipment, you can relax and do it all by the book. If using home-made expedients, watch the chicks carefully and observe how they are feeling. If they huddle together they are cold. If they desperately rush as far from the source of heat as possible, they are too hot.

Feeding and watering

Feeding and watering arrangements are the same as for chicks reared by a hen (see page 30). As the hen will not be there to

Geese *can* be aggressive.

Sheep folded with
hurdles on the lawn.

Hazel Pope and her
goats: note the rack for
greens. Hazel was about
to sheath the top of her
chestnut paling with
wire netting to prevent
harm to the goats.

teach the chicks to eat, you may have to show them how. Put out a dish of chick crumbs and 'peck' it sharply with a finger; the chicks will respond immediately and will not need to be shown twice.

Culling and slaughtering

It is not economic to keep laying hens more than two or possibly three years. Start to cull when the egg yield goes down. Fat hens are not generally good layers, so take them first. If you have not many hens, ring them with different coloured plastic leg rings (from the corn merchant again) and keep a note of which hens are laying.

Less reliable is the finger test: hold the hens in your left hand and measure with the fingers of the right hand the distance between the pelvic bones and the end of the breastbone; in full lay, these bones are up to a palm's width apart, with two to four fingers' width between the pelvic bones themselves. When a hen stops laying, the bones will be only a finger's width apart, and the pelvic bones will be close together.

I am squeamish about killing birds and have an ally who does it for me. But if there is no one else to do it, this is one way of doing it. Hold the hen's legs and wing-tips in your left hand. Hold her head with the first and second fingers of your right hand under her beak, and with the back of your hand lying on the back of her neck stretch her neck out over your right knee – don't pull, just extend it fully. A hard, sharp pressure just behind the back of her head will break her neck. You will feel the bones give. The wings will flap, but she will have died instantly.

Plucking and hanging

Country people say the bird should be plucked before it has stopped flapping. I do not work as quickly as that, but it is certainly much easier to pluck a bird while it is still warm. Keep the bird's head hanging down while you are working. Pull out the long quills from the tail and wings first. If keeping the feathers, collect the quills in a separate place. Then pluck the short feathers, working against the way they lie, from the neck, breast, thighs, wings and back. Hang the bird up by a string around its legs in a cool airy place away from flies. Hang it for two or three days before drawing.

Drawing

Lay the bird on its back, cut off the head and turn the bird over on to its breast. Slit the skin of the neck from the base to the end.

C

Pull the skin away from the neck and cut off the neck as close to the body as possible. Remove the crop and windpipe. Slit the skin from the vent to the parson's nose. Put two fingers of each hand inside the bird from each end and loosen the innards by sliding the fingers round, under the breast bone. Pull out the innards from the tail end gently, so as not to break the gall bladder, which would make the bird, and especially the giblets, taste bitter.

Discard the gut and the yellowish gall bladder, which will come out attached to the liver and should be removed with care. Keep the liver, the heart and the neck. Split the gizzard (which is the hard, rounded object) and wash out its inside; when it is clean, put it aside with the rest of the giblets.

Wipe the inside of the bird with a damp cloth, or wash it out with cold water. Slit the skin around the knee joints and twist the lower legs; they can then be removed by a sharp pull. Fold the flap of skin at the neck end under the back of the bird and tuck the wing-tips under to hold it there.

I find the birds cook better if not trussed – the legs are done at the same time as the breast.

DISEASE

Hens kept in hygienic conditions, fed fresh food in clean containers, allowed plenty of fresh water, fresh air and exercise, should remain healthy and hardy. The more space and freedom they have, the healthier they will be. However, certain things can go wrong. I have already mentioned insect pests and how to deal with them (page 29).

Digestive troubles such as diarrhoea are fairly common; if a hen has a mucky-looking vent she should be isolated for a few days in a warm coop and fed soft food, sparingly. Egg binding can also occur; the hen will be seen walking awkwardly, often visiting the boxes and straining uncomfortably. The treatment is to oil her vent with olive oil. If this does not work, hold her, vent downwards, in the steam from a bowl of hot water for about ten minutes. If this fails, get expert help or wring her neck. Crop-binding is caused by stringy foods, such as tough long grass or hay, matting together in the crop and causing congestion. The hen's crop becomes hard and enlarged and the bird looks dejected. Again, get expert help or wring her neck.

Lameness may be due to egg binding (see above) or to a swelling on the foot around a splinter, a corn or some injury. If the swelling is very large it is possible to lance it, keeping everything as clean as possible and painting the wound with iodine when the job is done. In milder cases, rest in a coop on soft litter for a few days may cause the swelling to disappear without further treatment.

The rules for the prevention of disease are:

1 Keep healthy stock under healthy conditions.
2 At the first sign of trouble, isolate any bird which looks off colour or loses its appetite.
3 If other birds become infected, or if the symptoms appear serious and unusual, call the vet.

Ducks

I have already pointed out some of the disadvantages of keeping these beguiling creatures but perhaps the chief worry is that those who once keep ducks become addicts: once a duck keeper, always a duck keeper. They are endlessly amusing and interesting to watch as they quest for food, gabbling quietly to each other.

Ducks are not usually the first choice of backyard egg producers and perhaps this is due to some popular misconceptions about ducks and their eggs. Ducks do not need a stream or a pond to swim in; they are quite content with a plastic bowl full of water, deep enough to bath in if possible, but at least deep enough for them to immerse their heads and bills to clean out their nostrils. Duck eggs are not poisonous. Their shells, being porous, can let in germs if the eggs are left lying in dirty, polluted places, but if the ducks are kept under clean conditions the eggs will be clean. To make doubly sure, the eggs should be thoroughly cooked.

Ducks eat a third more food than hens, as I've said already, but egg-laying breeds such as Khaki Campbells produce prodigious quantities of eggs, *large* eggs. During his undergraduate days, my husband Alan kept three ducks, which he fed on porridge and took with him everywhere, on holiday, on the Underground. You might suppose that this would put them off their lay, but every day he picked up six eggs from these three birds. He lived at this time on the banks of the River Cherwell, ideal duck territory, but today we frequently pick up more eggs in the morning than there are ducks, and our ducks are land-locked creatures with only a tub to swim in.

Ducks do little damage and much good in the garden – they get rid of slugs in a very short time – but they are not trustworthy with vegetables when these are tender and young, and they are

particularly fond of lettuce. However, a low fence will keep them
out of the vegetable garden.

WHERE TO BUY DUCKS

Watch the advertisements in a local paper, buy ducklings at
the feathered stage and rear them up. This is the way to be on
good terms with ducks, which are intelligent, long-memoried
and suspicious. They will form an integrated flock and stick together till death them does part.

Keep the ducks in for the first day or two until they feel at
home, and once the flock is formed it is a bad idea to add to it;
ducks are most reluctant to accept newcomers.

BREEDS

For eggs, choose Khaki Campbells or Indian Runners. Khaki
Campbells were originally bred by crossing mallard ducks with
Indian Runners, among others. They are brown, laced with buff;
small, light birds with long slim necks and heads; the drakes are
very handsome, with bronze or green heads, dark glossy backs
and pale grey underparts and curling tails. The Indian Runners
are usually of the white or black variety, but can also be choco-
late, fawn, or the spectacular fawn and white; they have an
extraordinary upright stance and do not waddle; when alarmed
they become so upright that they look like a row of rapidly
moving skittles. They have an air of great refinement with their
elegant heads and sloping shoulders and though even more nervous than most ducks, they are excellent layers.

There are other more unusual breeds such as the lovely Silver
Appleyards, Buff Orpingtons from my own area, the beautiful
Rouen ducks which look like stately, heavy versions of the wild
mallard, and the Muscovy ducks, which perch in trees and rear
their own young. But for heavy laying, I do not think you can
beat Khaki Campbells.

HOUSING

For much of the year ducks do not need any housing, but as
they must be protected from foxes we shut ours up at night. I have
often read that it is a mistake to keep ducks housed with hens. We
therefore had a separate house for the ducks, but we found that it
needed quite a lot of attention to keep it clean and pleasant. The
ducks now go in with the hens and their droppings are absorbed
into the deep litter which the hens turn and air daily. We have not
noticed any undesirable results from leaving the ducks and hens
together.

A duck house is easy to make. Ducks do not perch, do not need nesting boxes, do not use dustbaths; all they need is a roof, walls, floor and a door. (They dislike going through small openings and are distrustful of popholes.) Although water birds, they like the floor of their house to be dry, so they require litter (straw is the best); without the help of hens you will have to turn this every morning, adding fresh litter as necessary. Don't give them water at night; they will spill it in the litter. Proper ventilation will be good for the ducks and will help to keep the litter dry.

Ducks are best kept on free range, but can be perfectly happy kept in a run provided that they have been brought up to it. They will soon make their run messy, however. Allow at least 25 square feet of run space per duck, i.e., a space 5 feet by 5 feet. It is cruel to pen ducks that are used to their liberty. (For information on making poultry runs, see pages 25–6.) Provide shade and shelter in the run; ducks can suffer greatly from the heat.

DUCK MANAGEMENT

Ducks should lay before ten o'clock in the morning. This is the most opportune moment to let them out if, as is best, they are on free range. Feed them grain as for hens (see page 26) in the morning; put it in their water trough where only they can reach it (no wastage, no filching by the hens or wild birds) and where they will particularly enjoy it.

In the evening they will be ready for their mash or pellets (as for hens, see page 26). Give them as much as they want, up to say two handfuls each of dry weight. They will enjoy kitchen scraps, meat, fish and vegetables. Raw greenstuff is very much appreciated, and is essential when ducks are kept in restricted conditions. Chop it and drop it into their drinking water; then there will be no problem with driving them in at night. Like hens, they need flint grit and limestone grit or oystershell, which should be available at all times.

BREEDING DUCKS

Have only one drake for a flock of five or six ducks or there will be quarrels. He should not be related to the ducks. Ducks are not shy about mating, which generally takes place by or in the water with a great deal of quacking and head bobbing. If the drake is not active, get rid of him and find another.

Ducks are very poor mothers, indifferent both to their eggs and their offspring. To hatch the eggs it is essential to rely on broody hens or an incubator.

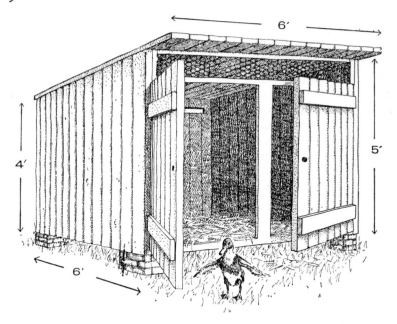

Duck house for six ducks. The front wire netting ventilator is 6 inches deep. Double doors make for easy cleaning. An inner, wire netting door on wooden frame should be fitted for summer use to give adequate ventilation; the wooden doors can then be left open. Rear view shows the 3-inch deep ventilator.

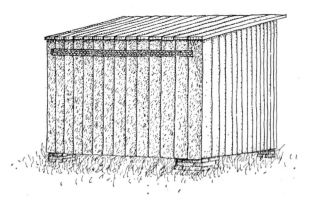

Rear view.

HATCHING DUCKS UNDER HENS

Collect eggs for a few days, up to a dozen per hen. Keep them in a cool place and turn them daily. Ducks' eggs must be kept damp while the hen is sitting, so put the coop or box on the earth or an upside-down turf, damp it and then make a nest of hay, if possible, or straw. Then continue as for hens' eggs but keep the eggs damp by sprinkling with warm water just before the hen goes back to the nest after her airing. The incubation period is twenty-eight days.

KEEPING DUCKLINGS WITH A HEN

Ducklings can be treated much as chicks but they must have water deep enough to wash their heads and bills. They must not be allowed to swim before they are two weeks old. They are always attracted to water and as they grow older, they can have a larger bowl of water with a brick or stone in it to help them get out after their splash.

ARTIFICIAL HATCHING AND REARING

The same principles apply to duck eggs and ducklings as to chicks (see page 32), although ducklings are hardier and will not require heat after the first week to ten days.

NOISE

Ducks quack. There is no getting away from the fact. Regular meal times will help to cut down the quacking and so will a calm relaxed life, so it is a good idea to stop children chasing them around. If neighbours still object to quacking, there is very little that you can do about it except to cease to keep ducks.

DUCKS FOR MEAT

Aylesburys are the best breed for table ducklings. They can be reared from day-olds with a brooder or from the feathered stage out of doors. They are ready for killing at ten weeks old; they should not be left longer than this or they will begin to moult and this will divert their energies from growing into feathering so that they lose condition; also the growing quills are a nuisance to pluck.

Spare drakes of egg-laying breeds should also be kept for meat. Though not bred as table birds, they are very good to eat, not fat but tender, gamey and full of flavour. If separated from the flock for fattening, they pine and will not eat, so we now leave them running with the others until they are of good size.

To kill a duck

Ducks should be killed in the same way as hens (see page 33).

Plucking and drawing

As for hens (see page 33). Duck down is of high quality and can be kept, washed and dried in the same way as goosedown (see page 44).

Disease

Ducks are remarkably healthy, on the whole. Occasionally one duck will be found to be ailing, probably due to some digestive trouble. Isolate the individual and hope for the best, but if she dies or has to be killed there is no reason to worry unduly unless other birds are also affected. If this happens, call the vet at once. My experience (and others have found the same) is that vets appear to be baffled in most cases by the ailments of ducks and also of geese, but that fortunately these ailments are few and far between. However, should there be any serious trouble the vet will send a corpse away for analysis.

The most common trouble with ducks is lameness, due to a painful swelling on the foot, or to sore feet in hard, dry weather. As a duck cannot bear to be alone, she will follow the others all day even when she is in agony, flopping down every few moments to rest, so the kindest thing is to put her on soft bedding, such as hay, in a coop. If possible, attach a little wire run to the coop, where she can be fed and where she can enjoy the grass, until the swelling subsides. This may take several days.

In the case of an injury, such as a broken wing, the vet is the proper person to consult.

Geese

Geese are now essential grass cutters in our once unmanageable garden. They cannot cope with large tough weeds but otherwise will keep grass as neat as a lawn; only occasional topping of docks, thistles and nettles will be necessary to discourage these to disappearing point.

The disadvantages of keeping geese are that they are very noisy and may be aggressive and that they cover the ground with their droppings. But in a garden where there is enough space to fence them away from the areas where people sit and where there are no neighbours to object to the cackling, geese are very well worth keeping.

How to start

The ideal is a breeding pen of two or three geese with one gander and enough grass to rear the goslings with a minimum of extra feed until Michaelmas. Then kill the young geese and put them into your freezer, or a friend's freezer, and sell any surplus at Christmas time. Traditionally, Christmas geese were put on the stubble and fattened on gleanings and grain, but to fatten geese on bought grain would be expensive for the garden-farmer and the extra money for the heavier goose would not, as I write, pay off. A green goose, that is one that has been reared mainly on grass, should weigh a minimum of 8 lb., more likely 10 lb. even for the lighter breeds, and that makes quite a meal for eight people before the giblet stew and the meals from the legs and wings. We have experimented with fattened geese and green geese and found fattening expensive. On the other hand, the slightly older goose has more flavour and we like to keep one or two a little longer. Goose freezes well if not kept too long; after about six months the flavour seems to deteriorate.

Housing

Geese need no shelter as they are very hardy, but they do need to be shut away from foxes at night. A handful of grain will bring them in at night. Ours spend the night in a portable wired-over run, which can be moved to a fresh patch each evening.

Sexing geese

There are many pitfalls to keeping geese and the first and chief is how to sex them. Geese are the arch-xenophobes and it is very difficult to persuade them to accept a newcomer, so it is important to get it right from the start. Our first year we bought twelve goslings. Our ally, the executioner, inspected them at the Michaelmas killing and assured us he had left us with a breeding pen – but alas, as it turned out we had no gander. The huge goose eggs were laid in vain as far as breeding went, though they made excellent custards and quiches. We imported a lonely two-year-old gander and also, after a fox's visit, another goose. The gander, perhaps through force of character, was accepted, but the strange goose suffered great miseries before her subsequent appearance on our table. The other geese refused to let her drink or feed; we tossed and turned at nights hearing her cries of distress from the run. After four months we decided to remove her but, so gregarious are geese, she still pined for her tormentors. In the end we had to kill her.

My advice would be to try to buy a mature breeding pen of geese. If this is impossible, buy goslings, keep quite a few, say six, through the winter, and observe them closely, trying to pick out the ganders. They are bigger than the geese, more aggressive and protective, stretch out their necks, keep between you and the other geese. You may see them mating in the early spring, but geese are shy about it. It is best not to breed from first-year birds anyway, as the goslings from older birds will be stronger.

BREEDING

By the second winter the pen should be established and any cases of mistaken identity sorted out. The geese generally start to lay in February. If left to her own devices, a goose will make a nest anywhere she fancies, but if the nest is unprotected she will be in great danger from foxes while she sits. It is better from January on to drive the geese into a fox-proof run each night and leave plenty of suitable nest-making materials around. The goose will make her own nest and proceed to lay a considerable number of eggs in it. Last spring we had a goose who finally sat on seventeen eggs.

These early eggs can be taken and put in an incubator or under a broody hen, if there is a broody hen so early in the year. Keep damping the eggs and remember that hens cannot turn them so they must be turned daily by hand. Mark them with a cross one side as for incubator eggs (see page 32).

The goose whose eggs were taken will lay a second batch of eggs. These too can be taken for incubation or she can be allowed to sit on them herself.

There are two reasons for trying to hatch so many goslings. First, goslings are quite tricky to hatch out and a man who does it professionally told me that he never expected more than a third of his goose eggs to hatch, so it is a good thing to aim at a surplus. Secondly, assuming that the garden-farmer will not have enough grass to rear large numbers of goslings, the day-old goslings can be sold at £1 each. When fully grown, say in June, £5 to £6 each would be the market price. At Christmas 1976 geese were selling in the shops at £1.50 per pound; the garden-farmer can do well by selling retail to people who like to know what they are getting, and from whom.

Help would be needed with the plucking and drawing (see page 33).

THE SITTING GOOSE

After laying a number of eggs, visiting them and turning them each day, the goose will show more and more reluctance to leave her nest and will eventually refuse to go out with the others in the morning. Leave grit and water available for her, and throw grain into the water where it will be ready if she wants it. Persuade her to leave her nest once or twice a day and damp the eggs for her, particularly towards the end of the thirty days' incubation. Goslings take a long time to chip through the shells but it is best to leave it to them and not to try to help.

The gander meantime will be pathetically bored and lonely without his wives. I read of one gander who collected a number of small thrown-out potatoes and sat on these while his mate sat on her eggs. It is best to keep him away during the actual hatching for he can be clumsy in his anxiety to help; when the goslings have been hatched for a day or two the family can be reunited.

Buy chick mash or chick crumbs which will give the goslings a good start in life and also provide much needed protein and vitamins for the mother. She will be in a poor state after sitting, and it will take her a month or so to recover condition.

Both ganders and geese are wonderful parents, fiercely protective. At any sign of danger the adult birds will form a ring around the babies and the gander has no fear of anyone or anything – so watch out and carry a stick at this time. As the goslings become less helpless the adult birds relax and become less aggressive.

Should the eggs fail to hatch it is perfectly possible to introduce day-old goslings to the mother goose for fostering. Buy the day-olds and put them in a warm place in a box covered with a blanket. Take care not to drop them or they will literally burst, being heavy and still having the egg yolk inside them on which they are feeding. Wait until dark and go out to the nest. The goose will hiss and then shift off her nest. Remove the eggs, put the goslings in the nest and then drive her gently back to them. Withdraw and leave them to it.

The goslings will pipe plaintively while the goose will hiss at finding strangers in her nest, but gradually the sounds will die down. Examine the nest with a torch after ten or fifteen minutes; the goose will hiss, but this time she will be hissing at you while the goslings will be snug under her feathers.

If for some reason she will not accept the goslings, they will have to be removed, for they would not survive very long in the cold night air, but I have not yet heard of a failure.

GRAZING AND FEEDING FOR GEESE

Geese do well on short grass, finding their keep even on sheep-nibbled pasture. They do a good job of keeping the grass down in an orchard without damaging the trees. They cannot, however, eat long, coarse grass and when we started we let two young geese die of starvation, not realizing that they were unable to eat the grass which was growing so abundantly.

Grass is the main food for geese and they cannot be healthy without it, but a handful of grain each in the evening will bring them into their run without bother, and keep them fit. Goslings need a supplementary feed of mash while they are growing. When the grass is not growing, between October and March/April, we give our geese a couple of handfuls each of mixed corn every day.

Water should be available at all times but they seem to like to find their own grit.

KILLING GEESE

Stun the goose unconscious with a blow on the head from a heavy spanner. Cut its throat with a knife at the base of the neck and bleed it for three minutes, after which time it will be dead.

PLUCKING AND DRAWING

This is quite a job and it is as well to share it with whoever is by. Keep the down in paper sacks; one day there will be enough for a pillow. The down should first be washed, and then dried either in a cool oven, loosely packed in paper bags, or hung up in net bags in a warm airy place for several days. Give the bags a shake from time to time to help the drying process.

The procedure for drawing is as for hens (see pages 33–4).

DISEASE

Geese are very hardy and it is extremely rare to lose an adult goose – except to a fox. Most of the troubles that can affect young birds, such as chills and diarrhoea, or insect pests such as lice, can be largely avoided by providing either very clean, good, dry housing, or none at all; making sure that any food given is fresh and fed in clean containers; and providing clean, fresh water. They may still pick up lice and it is a good thing to squirt them occasionally with an aerosol insecticide.

Slipped wing is a fairly common deformity, where the bird is unable to hold its wings close to its sides in the normal way. Never breed from a bird with this defect.

Worms can affect geese, particularly on land which has been heavily stocked with poultry for a considerable time. If the geese are losing flesh, consult the vet to see whether worms could be the cause; he will be able to provide a treatment.

Recipes

WHAT TO DO WITH THE EGGS OF HENS, DUCKS, AND GEESE

Soft-boiled and poached: Use the freshest of hens' eggs, never more than three days old.

Hard-boiled and stuffed: Duck eggs are the creamiest.

Scrambled and omelettes: Hens' eggs are the best for these, being the lightest and foamiest in texture.

Quiches, flans and custards: Goose eggs are excellent in these recipes, and so are duck eggs. One goose egg weighs approximately eight ounces (225 g.) and will make a perfect filling for a family-sized quiche, blended with cream or creamy milk and whatever combination of vegetables, cheese, ham, bacon, or herbs are to be used.

Try duck eggs for the most smooth and velvety crème caramel.

Meringues and soufflés: Hens' eggs must be used, for the whites of duck and goose eggs will not whip to the proper degree of stiffness.

Cakes and pastry: Duck and goose eggs can be used in any recipe which does not call for whipped egg-whites.

Soups, sauces and stuffings: All types of eggs are suitable, unless, as in mayonnaise, they are not to be cooked. In this case it would be unwise to use duck eggs.

Batters and pancakes: All types of eggs can be used; hens' eggs give a somewhat lighter texture to the batter.

Coping with the egg glut

There are various ways of preserving eggs. Only clean, perfect, uncracked eggs should be preserved; they will be suitable for all uses except boiling and poaching.

Preserving eggs in waterglass: It is very difficult to find waterglass in the shops in the plushy south-east. We buy ours in Scotland, where we spend our holidays. Once found, waterglass is easy to use. It is a glue-like substance sold in tins; make half a container of solution (the instructions are on the tin) and keep adding the fresh eggs daily. Leave the eggs covered by the solution until they are required. Do not use with ducks' eggs because of their porous quality.

In bran: For this method you will need a bag of bran (from the corn merchant) and a bottle of vegetable oil, as tasteless as possible. Corn oil is suitable.

Put a layer of bran in the bottom of a container. Smear the eggs with a thin film of oil, so that they are completely sealed, then put them in the bran, little end down; no egg should touch its neighbour. Cover each layer of eggs with a layer of bran. The eggs, if thoroughly oiled, will keep for many months stored in a cool dry place. But should the bran become damp, or, worst of all, should an egg break, the bran will begin to smell and will contaminate the eggs. So it is best not to put all your eggs, literally, in one basket but to have several smallish containers. The advantages of this method over waterglass are that bran and oil are more pleasant to use and easier to obtain.

In petroleum jelly and egg boxes: I have not tried this, but a friend recommended it; seal the eggs with petroleum jelly and pack them in egg boxes, after which they will keep for six months.

In cakes

Fruit cakes, rich in eggs, last for months, in tins or wrapped in foil. They are always welcome for picnics, good old-fashioned tea and replacement for a pudding at lunch-time. My mother-in-law makes the best rich fruit cakes I have ever eaten.

Eggs cannot be frozen whole, but sponge cakes store well in the freezer, and for anyone with children are a good way of making use of surplus eggs.

CAKE RECIPES

Special fruit cake (My mother-in-laws recipe)

12 oz. (350 g.) butter
9 oz. (250 g.) soft brown sugar
6 eggs
A few drops of vanilla, almond
    and coffee essences
3 tablespoons sherry or milk
Rind of ½ large lemon, grated
Rind of ½ large orange, grated
6 oz. (175 g.) glacé cherries,
    chopped

3 oz. (75 g.) almonds, chopped
15 oz. (425 g.) plain flour
¾ teaspoon salt
2 teaspoons mixed spice
18 oz. (500 g.) currants
15 oz. (425 g.) sultanas
9 oz. (250 g.) raisins
6 oz. (175 g.) mixed peel
3 tablespoons brandy

Line a large, deep cake tin with greaseproof paper. Cream the butter with the sugar until it is light and fluffy. Gradually add the lightly beaten eggs, one at a time, beating well between each addition. Beat in the essences, the milk or sherry, the orange and lemon rind, the chopped almonds and chopped cherries. Sieve the flour with the salt and spices; fold half of the flour with half of the fruit into the mixture. Add the remaining flour and fruit; stir well or mix with the hands.

Place the mixture in the tin. Smooth the top. Bake in a slow oven (300 °F/150 °C/gas mark 2) for about 3½ hours. If the top is browning too quickly, cover it with greaseproof paper.

Take the cake out of the oven and leave it to become completely cool. Then make several holes in it with a skewer and pour the brandy into the holes. Wrap the cake in foil and keep it for at least a month before eating it.

This mixture makes a dark rich, moist fruit cake, just right for Christmas or a birthday or any other special occasion.

Cherry cake

This cake is very good for picnics, or lunchtime or whenever anybody feels like a little something.

9 oz. (250 g.) butter
9½ oz. (265 g.) caster sugar (of
    which ½ oz. [15 g.] is for the top)
3 large eggs (or 4 small)
12 oz. (350 g.) self-raising flour

A pinch of salt
4–6 oz. (100–175 g.) cherries (of
    which a few are for the top)
1 tablespoon fresh lemon juice

Cream the butter with the sugar, keeping back ½ oz. (15 g.) for the top, until light and fluffy. Beat the eggs lightly and gradually add them to the mixture, beating well on every addition. Sift the flour with the salt. Quarter the cherries and mix them into the flour, keeping back a few cherries for the top. Fold the flour with cherries into the mixture, and add the lemon juice.

Put the mixture into a medium-sized, lined cake tin, smooth the top, sprinkle with the remaining caster sugar, arrange the remaining cherries on the top and bake for about 2 hours in a moderate oven (325 °F/170 °C/gas mark 3). Protect the top of the cake with greaseproof paper if it starts to brown too quickly during the latter stages of cooking.

CHICKEN RECIPES

Boiling fowl

There have been occasions with a really aged bird when I have had to admit defeat after many hours' cooking and fed the meat back to the cannibalistic hens, keeping only the soup for ourselves. Generally, however, an old hen makes a very good meal.

Chicken casserole

1 boiling chicken	6 peppercorns
Flour	2 cloves
Butter	Juice of 1 lemon
1 thick slice of bacon, cut into little cubes	Salt
	Parsley stalks
2 onions, sliced, or 8 whole shallots	Bay leaf
	Thyme
½ lb. (225 g.) carrots, quartered	Sliced potatoes (optional)
2 sticks of celery, sliced	Chopped parsley, to garnish
Stock or water to cover	

Joint the chicken, remove the yellow fat and set aside (see below). Set aside the giblets. Roll the pieces of chicken in flour and fry them gently in butter in a frying pan. When golden, pack into a casserole. Fry gently the cubes of bacon, onion rings or shallots, carrots and chunks of celery. Put all these around the chicken. Add stock or water to the juice in the pan, scraping and stirring the pan before pouring over the bird and vegetables. Add the peppercorns, cloves, lemon juice, salt, parsley stalks, bay leaf and thyme. Bring gently to the boil, cover tightly and leave, barely simmering, until the chicken is tender – say 2–2½ hours or even more, depending on the age of the bird. To make the dish more substantial, after an hour cover with sliced potatoes, well seasoned.

Towards the end of cooking, chop the giblets, fry the pieces very gently in a little butter and add them to the gravy. Garnish with chopped parsley.

Chicken fat: Put the pieces of fat in a pan with salt and a sliced onion. Leave covered on a very low heat until the fat has all melted leaving just crispy pieces of skin and onion. Strain into a bowl. It can be spread on bread instead of butter for the children's tea, or used for frying – it gives a delicious flavour to sautéd potatoes, fried bread and croûtons, mushrooms, etc.

DUCK RECIPES

Plump table ducks, such as Aylesburys, are best pricked all over with a fork, rubbed with salt and roasted on a grid; the fat should be poured off half-way through cooking. But if you keep and breed the lighter egg-laying ducks you will find that your surplus drakes are on the lean and gamey side, and it is best to treat them like wild ducks, buttering and basting them well and being careful not to overcook them. Thirty-five minutes roasting time should be enough for a small duck. Baby turnips are particularly good with roast duck. Skin them and put them round the bird so that they roast with it in the pan.

Duck with mint

1 young duck	2 tablespoons chopped mint
Bunch of mint	1 tablespoon redcurrant jelly
Butter or dripping	Salt
Juice of 1 orange	Pepper

Choose a young duck. Put a bunch of fresh mint into the cavity of the duck and roast in a moderately hot oven (400 °F/200 °C/gas mark 6) for up to about 40 minutes according to size, in good dripping or butter, or if plump in its own fat, basting frequently. Take out the duck and keep hot, removing the mint.

Make a stock with the giblets but do not use the liver. Cook the liver in a little butter, then pound it in a mortar until smooth. Add ½ pint (3 dl.) of stock to the juices in the tin and heat, stirring and scraping until it comes to the boil. Add it to the pounded liver, stir until smooth, then add the juice of the orange, the fresh mint and redcurrant jelly. Season with salt and pepper if necessary, put it in a sauce boat and serve with the duck.

Duck terrine

1 duck	Belly of pork
1 small wineglass fresh orange juice	Thyme
	Allspice
1 small wineglass brandy	Mace
Salt	1 egg
Pepper	Thin slices of pork fat

This is a good way of using an older bird. Carve thin slices from the best and most tender parts of the bird and marinate them

D

overnight in a mixture of the orange juice, brandy, salt and pepper. Take the rest of the meat from the duck, removing as many sinews as possible, and mince it finely, with some belly of pork, a third the weight of the meat from the duck.

Add herbs and seasonings to the minced meats and bind with an egg. Test for flavour by frying a tiny ball of it to taste.

Line a terrine dish with very thin slices of pork fat, then fill the dish with alternate layers of the minced meats and the slices of duck, starting and finishing with the minced meats. Cover with foil and put a pebble or two on the top of the foil. Stand the dish in a roasting tin, into which you have poured some hot water, and cook slowly in a very moderate oven (375 °F/190 °C/gas mark 5) for 1½ hours.

Allow to cool thoroughly, still covered by the foil, before eating or storing. It is best kept for at least one day before it is eaten. Serve with hot, crisp toast.

Storing terrines and pâtés: If you wish to keep a terrine or a pâté, seal with a thick layer of clarified butter or lard and it will keep in a cool dry larder for weeks. Alternatively it can be frozen. When making a terrine or a pâté for freezing, line the terrine dish with foil before continuing with the recipe. When cooked and thoroughly cooled, put the whole dish and its contents into the freezer for 24 hours. Then the food can be lifted out of the dish, in its foil, put into a polythene bag and put back into the freezer until required.

ROAST GOOSE RECIPE

Large plump geese are best cooked without a stuffing, in a way that gets rid of much of the fat. As with fat ducks, prick the goose all over with a fork, rub it with salt, put it on a grid in the roasting pan, so that the fat can drip down into the pan; pour off the fat half-way through cooking. Allow 10 minutes per lb./450 g. in a hot oven (450 °F/230 °C/gas mark 8). Serve with something sharp and tart to cut the richness – try crabapples poached whole in a syrup (½ lb. [225 g.] sugar dissolved in 1 pint [6 dl.] of water) flavoured with nutmeg, cinnamon and cloves and the juice and grated rind of a lemon.

Lighter breeds of geese, which have not been fattened, should be treated more like game. Stuff with a rather rich stuffing of the goose's liver, chopped and gently fried for a minute or two with chopped shallots. Add 4 oz. (100 g.) of liver sausage, 2 table-spoons of breadcrumbs, thyme, salt and pepper, and a tablespoon of brandy or Calvados. Soaked dried fruits, such as apricots or prunes, can be added. (Stone the prunes first!) Mix all together and stuff the goose; then roast in a moderate oven (350 °F/ 180 °C/gas mark 4) for about 10 minutes per lb.4/50 g., being careful not to overcook.

The giblets make a very good separate dish for another day. Casserole them with stock from the goose carcass, a tin of tomatoes, plenty of garlic and onions and a ½ lb. (225 g.) piece of pork.

The fat should be carefully kept for it is quite delicious for frying, or as a seal for terrines and pâtés.

CHAPTER TWO

Sheep

FOR SHEEP you must have a large garden, effective fencing, a certain amount of expertise, some physical strength and time to visit them daily. They will almost inevitably escape and will probably hoover up precious vegetables as they move at a brisk trot through the garden. When they have lambs with them they make quite a lot of what we, though perhaps not others, consider a rather pleasant noise.

On the bonus side, they will graze, manure and trample with their sharp little feet until the roughest patches of grass become smooth as lawns. They do not touch bulbs or damage the bark of trees (although they will crop low-hanging branches) so those who have an area of rough grass in their gardens, perhaps an old orchard planted with daffodils and snowdrops, which might include steep banks which are awkward to mow and ditches which need clearing, would find sheep eager and willing garden tidiers.

To take advantage of the meat it is essential to have a freezer – or rather almost essential, because the meat could be salted, or you could give a huge party and dispose of the whole lot in one evening, but a freezer is obviously the most practical way to store the meat. The lambs should be killed once they have reached a weight of about 100 pounds, probably in July or thereabouts; this should give about fifty pounds of superb meat. Our lambs, which subsist on all sorts of herbs, flowers and twigs which would not be tolerated for a moment by a farmer, taste far more like Scotch or Welsh lamb than the fat and succulent, but less tasty, English farm lamb.

The ewes can be kept on after the lambs have gone, either in the garden, in which case you will have to arrange for them to go to the ram in October, or running with the flock of a friendly farmer until point of lamb in the next spring. In all but the largest gardens there will not be enough grass to provide winter keep for the ewes. If it is impossible to board them out for the winter, they will have to be sold when the grass stops growing in the autumn, or at the time that their lambs are disposed of. Alternatively, you can put them too into the freezer. I am bound to admit that I have not done this myself, but crofters in the Hebrides do it and so no doubt do other farmers. I am told that the mutton is good if carefully cooked and, as old ewes fetch poor prices in the autumn, it might be worth a try.

How much land?

It would not be worth keeping sheep on less than an acre of good grass; in a normal year this should keep two ewes and their lambs through the summer. In times of drought, such as we have had in recent summers, they will need a supplementary source of food; perhaps a neighbour with a patch of grazing would help you out (see Chapter 9 for grass management). Sheep are not fussy about what they eat so long as it is vegetable; they will accept stale bread, apple cores, garden waste, tree prunings, wilted nettles or, of course, bought concentrates or corn. However, one hopes that they will thrive on grass alone, with extra food kept strictly for treats.

Poisonous plants

Most people know that yew is deadly poisonous. Laurels are also poisonous and should be cleared from the paddocks where sheep are kept. Acorns are poisonous to sheep (and horses, though not to pigs, for some reason) but probably the sheep will not eat them in large enough quantities to do harm. However, if the sheep look sickly and you have seen them tucking into acorns it would be as well to move them and call the vet.

Brambles, though not poisonous, are a nuisance because the sheep are apt to tangle themselves up in the briars.

How to start

Fencing
   This is the major item of expense and there is no perfect
alternative except to dig a moat and fill it with water. This is the
system used on Romney Marsh, where the sheep are very satisfactorily confined by dykes, and all the farmer has to do is to gate
the bridges.
   Whatever fencing is used must be strong, as sheep are adept at
escaping. I have watched a ewe examining the fence inch by inch
until she found a point where the wire was slack; she then
patiently worked away at the bottom until she could lever up the
wire enough to squeeze underneath. Several strands of barbed
wire stretched tightly between stout firm posts will do the trick;
it must be done with a wire-strainer and a 'drivall' or a sledge
hammer for driving in the posts (see the illustrations on pages
130–1). A drivall looks like a huge, two-handled metal jug. It is
very heavy. Stick the post into the ground, put the head of the
post into the drivall and drop the drivall down over the post,
repeating until it is firmly driven in. Choose a time when the
ground is not too hard to drive in the posts securely. A home-
made wire-strainer can be made from a three-foot length of metal
piping. Make a saw-cut across the diameter of the pipe at one end
to a depth of three inches and wide enough to admit the wire.
The pipe can be used as a lever against the posts to stretch the
wire taut; then secure the wire to the posts with staples (see the
illustration on page 130). The job is easier with two people, but
can be done alone.
   This sort of fencing, however, is expensive and ugly. The same
can be said of chain-link fencing, which is also effective. We use
the less obtrusive, but much more frail, sheep netting on chestnut
posts, with one strand of barbed wire along the top to discourage
climbers. Even this is quite expensive, and it will not last indefinitely as the posts will eventually rot and the wire netting
will weaken.
   Rolls of cleft paling are prettier (see the illustration on page
131), but the teeth at the top have to be sheathed in doubled-over
netting, or the sheep may hang themselves and die; this fencing
again is far from cheap. Hurdles I would not recommend as they
are even more expensive and do not last very long, but a few are
useful for penning sheep in a corner for a short time or for use as
emergency gates or stopping a hole in the fence.
   The best compromise for the garden-farmer is probably sheep

or pig netting with a strand of barbed wire along the top and possibly along the bottom as well. Sheep benefit from being moved on from time to time, and so does the grass, so two or three small paddocks, if possible adjoining each other for easy moving, would be the best arrangement.

A right of way through the grazing can lead to problems. Walkers are quite unscrupulous about pulling up wire fences to allow their dogs underneath, if the dogs are too heavy to lift over the stiles you have thoughtfully provided, and where a Labrador can go a sheep will follow. It is better to provide wicket gates and paint on a prominent 'Please shut the gate' notice.

Tethering

This year I experimented very successfully with tethering a ewe. My equipment was an iron crowbar, a heavy iron chain, a large leather dog-collar and a stout metal mallet encouragingly named 'Thor'. The ewe was moved daily, to a different one of those awkward corners of the garden which are so difficult to keep tidy. She did a particularly fine job on an ex-rockery and she also smartened up the bases of the hedges. In dry weather we gave her a bucket of water, but in damp weather when the grass was juicy she did not drink.

When we put her out with a neighbouring flock for tupping (going to the ram) she was pathetically reluctant to let me leave her. I left her attempting to clamber over the stile after me. When I walked through the field she came at my call and I always had to carry something for her in my pocket, such as a piece of bread, an apple, or a Polo mint – which she adores. She was and is a most appealing companion, allowing Flora, my five-year-old daughter, to ride on her woolly back or snuggle against her flank as she lies down to chew the cud.

Housing

Sheep need no housing, but newborn lambs may need shelter in bad weather.

Water

Water should always be available for the sheep to drink. They will probably not drink if the grass is sappy and the weather normally damp, but in times of drought they will drink quite a lot, particularly if the lambs are suckling. Without piped water a considerable amount of fetching and carrying is necessary, and this should be taken into account when planning the paddocks.

Lambing

The information for these diagrams is taken from *The Complete Book of Self-Sufficiency* by John Seymour (Faber and Faber). Normally a ewe gives birth unaided standing up. But if the birth is prolonged for more than an hour, she will need assistance.

If no vet or skilled person is available, lay the ewe on her back, propping her up with a bale of straw.

Wash your hands and the hindquarters of the ewe, before lubricating your hand and her vulva with boiled linseed oil or carbolized oil.

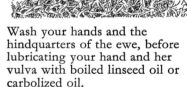

If the forefeet of the lamb have been visible for an hour, tie a soft cord round the feet, pulling gently when she strains. However, if you cannot see any sign of the lamb appearing, very carefully insert your hand into the ewe while she is not straining.

If the lamb is in the correct position for a normal birth, take hold of its forelegs and gently begin to pull.

Pull strongly when the ewe is straining, but don't
when she isn't.

Support the lamb's body as it appears with your free
arm, twisting it slightly when it is half out to relieve
the pressure.

Finally, clean the newly born lamb's nostrils of any
mucus, before allowing the mother to start licking her
latest offspring.

Buying stock

A kindly sheep farmer is an almost essential friend for the amateur. He may let you have a couple of his own old ewes, or he may be able to find them for you elsewhere.

The best time to buy the ewes, if they are only wanted during the grass-growing season, is just before they lamb. February/March would be a good time, for the garden-farmer would probably not want early lambs. Some farmers like to have them early because of the high price the lambs will fetch, but if you want to feed the sheep on surplus grass and later have the meat for the freezer, there is no point in having early lamb and paying for it by feeding hay or concentrates.

Management

Lambing

This, with old ewes, should not be a problem and we have not yet had to follow the instructions on the diagrams (pages 56–7). But should a ewe be in labour for some time, say an hour or two, or seem distressed, the best thing would be to get the vet or ask the help of someone who is experienced. It would be very unwise for an unsupervised amateur to try to feel inside the uterus or to pull out a lamb. If the weather is reasonable and the paddock not too exposed, the ewe should be able to look after the lamb or lambs in the open. Windbreaks are worth putting up if there is no sheltered place; hurdles or straw bales can be used. If there is a bitter wind, or if the lambs look weakly, they can be put into a shed with the ewe for a day or two. Little polythene jackets are now sold for newborn lambs; a farmer might be able to provide some or perhaps one could make them out of plastic bags. The bags wrap around the lambs' bodies with holes cut out for head, legs and tail.

Foxes have been known to take young lambs, so it is prudent to keep them as close to the house as possible while they are tiny.

Veterinary treatments

As the investment in sheep is quite large, it would be rash to skimp on these. The vet will, if asked, do all the treatments listed for you, but that would naturally bump up expense. Should a lamb need treatment from the vet near to killing time, make this clear to the vet; the last thing you want is a carcass full of antibiotics.

Injections: Newborn lambs have a routine injection soon after birth to protect them against pulpy kidney, lamb dysentery and tetanus. Use a hypodermic syringe and inject under the skin. The vet will supply a bottle which contains several treatments. The syringe should be sterilized before use.

Castration: Male lambs should be castrated a week after their jabs. This is to make them fatten faster. It is quite painless then and simply involves putting a rubber ring (from the vet) around the testicles as close to the body as possible. A special pair of pliers is used to stretch the ring and enable it to slip on easily. The part beyond the ring then atrophies.

Tail docking: The lambs' tails are docked at the same time and in the same way as castration, with the same rubber rings and pliers.

Worming: Sheep and lambs are very subject to parasites and it is a good thing to treat them with a drench, perhaps half-way through the summer or if they do not seem to be thriving. The drench is bought from the vet in powder form and mixed with water before being administered.

For drenching, two people are needed: one holds the animal while the other puts his thumb in the side of its mouth to hold it open, and then pours the drench down the animal's throat, through the side of its mouth, from a bottle.

Foot rot: Sheep are rather prone to this unpleasant infection. Act quickly at the first sign of limping or discomfort. A sharp pen-knife is quite adequate for cutting away the rot. The foot should then be sprayed with an aerosol foot spray containing an antibiotic treatment; this can be bought from the vet.

Shearing

This can be done, as a friend of mine saw it being done recently in Kashmir, with an old pair of scissors, but it is better to ask the farmer who supplied the sheep if he would be willing to shear the ewes with his own in return for the fleeces; each fleece is worth about £4 at 1976 prices. Shearing is done in May in the south and later in the north. The lambs should not be shorn if they are to be killed, as shearing diminishes the value of the fleece later. If sheep are not shorn they lose their wool naturally; they look very strange with half their fleece hanging off, but seem quite happy with the arrangement.

Handling and catching sheep

Without a sheepdog this can be very tricky. There is only one answer: make the sheep thoroughly tame by feeding them daily with something they like. Very soon the ewes lose all fear; they can be stroked and petted, will eat from your hand and follow you everywhere.

Transport

Sheep are agile creatures and can nip into the back of a van or estate car, lured by something edible. A grid, as used by owners of large dogs, will stop them joining you in the driving seat, otherwise some reasonably strong person will have to travel with them in the back.

Do sheep pay?

A costing of our sheep enterprise, 1975, may be of interest. The ewes at point of lamb cost us £10 each. We averaged three lambs from every two ewes. The average weight of lambs at killing time was 90 lb., providing about 45 lb. of meat per lamb. It was a very dry season and grass was short. Allowing £1 per lamb for veterinary treatments, £1 for the food used for taming and bribing and £3 per lamb for the cost of butchering and preparing for the freezer, then subtracting the autumn sale price of the ewes (£7 to £8 per ewe) the figures look like this:

Costs per ewe:

	£	p
Purchase price	10.	00
Vet treatments per 1½ lambs	1.	50
Food per 1½ lambs	1.	50
Butchering 1½ lambs	4.	50
	17.	50

Gains per ewe:

	£	p
Sale price	7.	00
Meat of 1½ lambs @ 50p per lb.	33.	75
	40.	75
Plus fleece if sold	4.	00
Total	£44.	75

This costing makes no allowance for fencing or labour costs. On the other hand, it makes no allowance for saving on other forms of keeping grass down, such as mowing, petrol and the service of machinery. Once the problem of fencing has been solved, and assuming that the sheep are properly looked after so that there are no losses through neglect, keeping sheep is financially very attractive.

Recipes

LAMB RECIPES

Roast lamb

1 leg or shoulder of lamb	1 tin of tomatoes
Garlic	Green vegetables in season
Thyme	Salt
Rosemary	Pepper
2 onions, sliced	3 tablespoons fresh cream or
3 carrots, sliced	1 egg yolk
1 glass red wine	¼ pint (1½ dl.) milk

My favourite way of roasting a joint of lamb is to push slivers of garlic into the meat near the bone, sprinkle the joint with thyme and rosemary and put it into the pan on a grid. Under the joint go sliced onions, sliced carrots and more garlic. Put it into a hot oven (450 °F/230 °C/gas mark 8) for twenty minutes, then add a glass of red wine and a small tin of tomatoes with the juice. Continue roasting, allowing twenty minutes per lb./450 g., and checking that the vegetables are not sticking or burning, adding more liquid if necessary. Put the meat on a dish and keep it hot.

Put the contents of the roasting tin into a saucepan. Take green vegetables in season, such as peas, runner beans or broad beans, and add them to the gravy and vegetables to cook. Taste to see that the seasoning is right. Add some fresh cream before serving, or beat the yolk of an egg in ¼ pint (1½ dl.) of milk, add the gravy to the milk and egg a little at a time, stirring well, then return it to the pan, stir and leave on a very low heat until the mixture has thickened, stirring occasionally.

Plain boiled rice and a green salad are all anybody could want with this dish.

Blanquette d'agneau

This recipe is unorthodox but good and I think better than the usual white stew, with a sauce thickened with flour as well as egg and cream. This sauce is thickened only with fresh cream and egg yolks.

1 lb. (450 g.) cubed shoulder of lamb	Oil
	Salt
Thyme	¼ pint (1½ dl.) stock
Parsley	Lemon juice
White pepper	1 egg yolk
Garlic	¼ pint (1½ dl.) cream
Butter	

Trim all fat from the meat and cut into largish cubes. Sprinkle the meat with fresh thyme, chopped parsley, freshly ground white pepper and crushed garlic. Cook it very gently in a very little butter and oil in a heavy pan. Keep an eye on the meat to see that it is cooking really slowly. After 10 to 15 minutes add salt, lemon and stock, and taste to see that the balance of herbs and seasoning is right; it should taste very savoury and fragrant. Cover and continue to cook until tender.

Prepare some boiled rice and a green salad to have with the blanquette.

When the meat is tender, lift it out with a slotted spoon and put it in a serving dish, surrounded by the rice. Keep it all warm. Beat up an egg yolk, add ¼ pint (1½ dl.) of cream and, off the heat, add this mixture to the meat juices in the pan. Stir in a double saucepan until the sauce coats the back of the spoon, strain the sauce, taste to check the seasoning, then spoon some of the sauce over the meat and serve the rest separately.

MUTTON RECIPES

I must come out into the open and say that we have never tried to cook old mutton, but I am told that this is how it is done.

Marinade for mutton

The mutton should be well hung. Marinade it before cooking for two or three days as follows:

2 onions	1 pint (6 dl.) water
2 carrots	1 clove of garlic
2 sticks of celery	Salt
1 teacup oil	Pepper
½ pint (3 dl.) red wine	Parsley
¼ pint (1½ dl.) wine vinegar	Rosemary

Chop the onions, carrots and sticks of celery. Fry them in the oil. When they are browned, add the red wine, wine vinegar, water and a crushed clove of garlic, salt, pepper, parsley, and rosemary; bring it all to the boil, simmer for half an hour, and then take it off the heat. Leave it to become completely cold.

Put the mutton into a deep dish, pour over the marinade, turn the mutton about in the marinade and leave it in a cool place, turning the meat over from time to time to allow the marinade to soak into every part.

When you are ready to cook the meat, take it out of the marinade, wipe it and proceed according to the recipe you are following.

Roast mutton

For roasting, old mutton should be wrapped in foil and cooked in a very slow oven (275 °F/140 °C/gas mark 1) for three or four hours. The foil should then be removed and the heat turned up to hot (450 °F/230 °C/gas mark 8), and the cooking continued until the joint is brown, basting frequently.

Boiled mutton

For boiling, allow 30 minutes per lb. (350 g.). Brown the marinaded piece of meat in dripping then put it in a suitably large pan, add carrot, a turnip, an onion, a stick of celery; cover with water or stock, add herbs and seasoning, put on the lid and let the meat simmer gently.

The vegetables will not be good to eat after lengthy cooking. Have a purée of potatoes with the mutton, or haricot beans, and braised carrots and turnips.

Caper sauce is traditional with boiled mutton. Make a white sauce with butter and flour, adding half stock, half milk; season, flavour with Dijon mustard and a little vinegar and leave to simmer for a little while; add capers and a dash of cream and the sauce is ready.

Tenderizing mutton

Freezing is said to tenderize mutton. Some people beat the meat with a rolling pin before cooking.

CHAPTER THREE

Goats

IN MY childhood, anybody who kept goats was regarded with
considerable suspicion. Goats smell, and therefore so do their
owners, we were told. I had a general impression that goats' milk
was strong and distasteful and was only drunk by their poverty-
stricken owners and some invalids who, poor things, could not
tolerate cows' milk.

It was not until my children went to school that I met their
teacher, Hazel Pope, who is as unlike my childhood picture of a
goat-keeper as the goats themselves are unlike the terrifying and
smelly bogies I imagined. Hazel lives in a house and garden
which I could never have thought would sustain goats, rather
smaller than many suburban plots and with close neighbours on
either side. She has a full-time job and three school-age children
to look after and still finds time for cooking and dressmaking as
well as many other things. She makes the most delicious goats'
cheese (the recipe is on pages 74–5), eagerly wolfed down by those
who do not know what it is. I think it was this cheese that
convinced me that goats' milk, far from being second-best, is in
fact a luxury and I asked her to contribute her experience to this
book.

HOW TO START

Hazel Pope writes:

Any garden that can take a shed roughly ten feet square leading into a yard of similar size is big enough to keep a couple of goats in.

So if you have already planned a highly intensive and productive vegetable garden, which may well lead off the back lawn towards the bottom fence where you probably have an efficient compost heap and a bit of spare ground, or perhaps a greenhouse and a garden shed, then go and stand down there and consider: 'Could we keep a goat?'

Now, if you decide that there is room, and that you are not going to construct or adapt something that might cause neighbourhood disapproval or contravene any local bylaws (see Chapter 12), you can start to think constructively. First of all you will have to keep two goats – one on her own would become lonely and depressed. Then you must resolve to keep them well-housed, correctly fed and clean. Living like this goats can be healthy, productive and quiet. They are far less offensive than the dog that barks all day shut in the kitchen, or the cat that scratches in your carefully prepared seed bed.

Once you have decided that your garden can cope with your animals, you must give serious thought to your own nature and temperament. If you are not used to handling animals, a goat is a good introduction. She is, when handled with love and respect, and not a little firmness, rarely the capricious, butting creature that appeared in the comics of our childhood. She is intelligent, responsive and affectionate, and as well as becoming a household pet will repay all your care and attention by inundating you with milk.

The decision made, seek the advice of local goatkeepers before rushing to buy shed, equipment or goats. The British Goat Society will give you addresses of goat owners in your area, and you will probably be surprised to discover how many there are, and even more surprised at their friendliness and willingness to help.

You will find there are many different methods of housing goats, and many adaptations of the ideal, but gradually you will absorb all the information and arrive at a system which suits your special needs; one which suits your garden and is planned in a time- and labour-saving fashion to suit your daily routine. You will have seen many different breeds of goat and decided which

E

breed you prefer. Your choice should be influenced by your method of husbandry; it is not really fair to keep an animal used to free range in a yard.

Some breeds are more adaptable than others, though breeders seldom agree which they are. Goats are browsing animals, never happier than when up on their hind legs, with their faces buried in a hedge in fastidious search of the choicest shoots. But some breeds will graze the lawn for you too. Without doubt most goat-keepers will agree that, as far as milk production goes, any breed of goat reared and kept intensively can be more productive than one free range. This is possibly because the energy that would have been used in foraging for food has been diverted to milk production.

All the planning becomes very exciting, and one dreams of coming in at the back door at dawn with a bucket of frothing milk. This all sounds most bucolic and romantic. The truth is often very different, and may mean that you come in out of the rain with a temperature of 102° scarcely able to ask yourself how you ever became involved in all this bother just so that you could cancel your local dairyman, and play at being independent. So you must ask yourself a few more questions before taking the final plunge.

First, are you prepared or able to milk regularly, 365 days a year, morning and evening, in sickness and in health? Is someone in the family willing to learn to milk for you if you are really too ill to be outside? You must be absolutely sure that you are covered by a second in command, whether family or willing friend.

Then, of course, there are the holidays. Some enthusiasts take their goats with them, but most board them out with a reliable goat-keeper. In your original search for help and advice you will have met someone who will board your goats for you, generally for much less than it would cost to board a cat or dog. If you are used to booking your holidays early in the year, then it is a simple matter to book your goats' holiday at the same time. If you leave it to the last minute you will have difficulties, especially at popular holiday times.

If you are still undaunted by the nature of the responsibilities you are about to undertake, then read thoroughly all the literature on the goat that you can find. If still undaunted, especially by the list of ailments, and also remembering that most books demonstrate the ideal, which you will have to adapt, your dreams can gradually become reality.

It may help those unused to keeping animals and therefore

unwilling to commit themselves too eagerly to the task to follow the fortunes of one who hesitated for years, mainly because the garden was thought to be too small, and then because no one in the family had any do-it-yourself ability in the garden beyond putting up a wavy and collapsible chicken run.

No one could have been more interested or more hesitant. No local agricultural show was missed, leaflets were collected, and goats were admired. Years passed under the mistaken, as it turned out, impression that it would be necessary to move in order to keep goats – especially since a friend had expressed horror at the thought of keeping the animals in any area less than an acre, and the garden concerned was certainly less than half that.

Then a combination of fortunes coincided, not the least of which was having £200 to spend, the more unmentionable being a fortieth birthday, which engendered a defiant attitude towards time. With this impetus the following sequence of events ensued.

First the British Goat Society was approached. They sent the addresses of goat-keepers in the locality. These were duly visited and quizzed, happy to show their goats and defend their various systems of husbandry. An enormous amount of information was amassed over several months, which resulted in two British Toggenburg female goatlings being bought, but left with their patient owner until their new living quarters were ready.

At the same time a prefabricated double pony stable was bought through the 'for sale' column in the local paper, along with several calf pens, which seemed ideal for sectioning off one stable into two goat pens.

Whilst all this was being organized, all the detritus of years of family life was collected – old bike frames, pram bases, and such rubbish. Local dumps were raided, and when enough scrap had been collected it was laid out as hard core along with some builders' rubble, in an area the size of the shed. This area had already been dug out to a depth of about six inches to take the concrete base. All this preparation was from the advice of goat-keepers who also gave the proportions for concrete mixing, and the yardage required for the area.

The laying and screeding of the concrete and indeed the erection of the sectional shed itself was one of those prolonged nightmares from which many useful lessons were learned: never leave fresh concrete unprotected in frosty weather – it was February; never attempt to erect a shed until the mortar supporting the breeze blocks on which it will rest has hardened, or the breeze blocks will fall over and so will the shed; be sure the bituminous felt which covers the roof is carefully and securely fixed before you even stop for a cup of tea or the wind will rip it off and take it across the garden like an enormous flying carpet.

A word about the breeze blocks. These were laid – as suggested by the vendors of the shed – on their long sides. This gave a height of nine inches allowing for a depth of bedding if deep litter was going to be used. Additionally a couple of drainage holes were made in those at the back of the shed. The concrete itself had been laid 'to fall' – that is, to slope slightly towards these holes.

Then one of the stables was sectioned off with the calf pens into two pens and a handling area. The door of this stable led into a yard about ten feet square, which had a gate into the garden. There was a connecting door between the two stables, as the second one was to be used as a hay and food store, and also as a milking area, since it is better not to milk in the living quarters. Hay-racks were made out of scraps of weld-mesh. These soon proved too small, and were later replaced by a double hay-rack, specially made to sit on the dividing wall between the two pens, thus serving them both. It needed a lid, which was made out of an old vegetable rack, since goats are good at dragging all the hay out on to the floor as they look for what they consider to be the best bit. They will do this in any case, but a lid lowers the wastage.

Most goat-keepers hang their water buckets by chains from the wall of the pen. It is well worth buying a heavy-duty plastic bucket with a strong metal handle to clip on to the chain. Goats are heavy drinkers, and like warm water, especially in the winter. The bucket needs a good wash-out at least once a week, as it soon gets a slimy film in it. Goats are fussy creatures, and won't drink from a dirty bucket or eat anything that has been on the floor of the stable or yard.

Feeding buckets need to be metal, and firmly set in holders if food is not to be wasted. A goat will carry a loose bucket about, and if it is plastic she will also attempt to include it in her diet.

Against one of the fences in the yard is another hay-rack, made out of a baker's wire basket found on a dump, for feeding greens and hay. The yard itself was made from concrete paving stones, once a garden path.

Before the yard was quite finished the goats arrived, and had to stay in their shed until the fence and gate were firmly fixed – or so we thought.

The great moment for letting them into their yard arrived. The door was opened. When we first let them into the yard, they shot out, hackles up, and straight over the fence into the garden, where they stood trembling with terror. They were in fact very nervous little animals, and unused to being handled. The fence, chestnut paling, which was a bad choice since it can be dangerous, was extended to five feet by means of a wire, and has since been modified with wire netting to make it safe by sheathing the spiky top in wire mesh. (For different kinds of fencing, see the relevant section of Chapter 2 on sheep, and the illustrations on pages 130–1.)

Eventually the animals settled down. One of them arrived in kid, and duly had one male, which was taken to the vet to be put down. One of the least attractive aspects of keeping goats is disposing of unwanted kids. Never keep male kids for breeding; leave this to the expert breeder whose aim is to select for stud. Kids can be reared for meat if one doesn't need the milk for the house and is not too sentimental. Female kids are a different matter, but difficult decisions have still to be made which must not be governed by sentiment. At all times you must try to make your goat-keeping as economical as possible for the returns you get in the way of milk and its by-products. If you are only keeping two goats, then you will have one milking and one 'running through'. Goats milk for two years after kidding, which means they would be mated alternate years. The one 'running through' is the one in the second year of her milking, approaching mating during the autumn and subsequent kidding five months later. She will only need to be 'dry' for about six weeks before she kids.

BREEDING

It is generally quite obvious when a goat is in season. She becomes restless, bleats hopefully most of the time, and wags her tail. She will come into season during the autumn months once every three weeks, and will be in this restless state for three days. It is well to take her to the male as soon as the signs are noticed, because the male is much more interested in her as her season commences, and there is nearly always a successful mating. If three weeks later she 'returns', then she must in fact be returned to the male, for which there is no second fee.

Sometimes a goat does not come into season at all, and has to be persuaded to do so. You then take a piece of old rag to the stud goat, whereupon his owner will rub it on the scent glands on his head. Back you go to your impassive goat, who will change in demeanour as soon as she gets wind of what to you is an offensive article. Each time you visit her you let her have a close sniff of the lovely thing, leaving it where it can still be smelled but not reached in the meantime. Within a day or two she will come into season.

ROUTINE

A regular routine is good both for yourself and the goats, even if you have plenty of time for everything. Generally speaking you must allow yourself an extra twenty minutes at either end of the day on top of what you already do. Then the goats will have accommodated themselves to your daily pattern. Of course, the more time you spend with your animals the tamer and happier they become, you learn much more about their habits, become more observant about their general health, and a much better goat-keeper. But if you are at work during the week they will have to do without the extra loving until the weekend.

You will find a routine to suit yourself, but the following may be of some help, being the daily routine of a family of two adults and three children, all of whom are out all day, home at weekends and school holidays. The morning is perhaps the most worry, since goats know nothing of buses and trains, and if there should be a small crisis, there ought to be time allowed to deal with it.

7 a.m. – 7.40 – Breakfast and make sandwiches for children's lunches.
7.45 – Feed and water goats and hens, clear up breakfast, get ready for work.
8.10 – Milk goats, let them into the yard, check all catches and fastenings (this becomes second nature), strain and cool milk.
8.30 – Leave for work.

After this the rule is that whoever arrives home first in the afternoon feeds the goats greens or branches. The evening feeding and milking routine can be more relaxed, but should take place roughly twelve hours after the morning milking. At weekends and holidays the goats can be tethered in the garden and often taken for walks, when they are able to browse on the hedges and verges.

FEEDING

Goats need a food ration which provides for body maintenance and milk production. The amount for maintenance varies with the age and size of the goat and whether or not she is in kid. The amount for milk production depends on the milk yield. No amount of high-quality feeding will improve the yield of a low-producing goat, one who would be described as a poor milker, whereas a goat whose milk yield is gradually increasing would have her rations increased to meet her needs.

Feeding can be difficult for the novice to understand, since there are so many points to be considered – the main ones being the special requirements of each animal, the system of husbandry, and the quality and type of food available. It has become a complicated affair because the aim of serious goat-keepers over the years has been to breed high-yielding dairy goats – those who will produce nine pints and more over a twenty-four-hour period. For a small animal to do so well, the feeding must be finely and carefully balanced. Much better for the beginner to settle for an animal likely to produce less than this, perhaps five to seven pints a day, where errors in feeding might not be too disastrous. A badly fed high-potential goat will continue to try to keep up her production to the disadvantage of her general health. The person who sells you your goats will give you their menu, and any alterations in diet you need to make to suit your methods should be made gradually.

Concentrates have therefore to be fed wisely, since they will improve and support the milk yield of your goat up to her maximum, but can be reduced if you are feeding hay of good protein content, or any proteinaceous greenstuff.

They are called concentrates because they lack fibre and water and are therefore not bulky, consisting of foods such as flaked maize, broad bran, rolled oats, locust bean pods, and linseed cake, providing starch and protein. They can be bought from the corn-merchant in ready-made mixtures called dairy nuts or meals, but many goat-keepers have their suppliers make up a mixture for them, often because they find their goats object to the fishmeal content of some of the ready-mixed brands.

As well as concentrates you will need to buy hay. The goat is a ruminant which means she can digest bulky fibrous foods, eating it as it is available, and cudding it at her leisure. There are various types of hay, and as you gain more experience you will learn to recognize the best for your animals. The need for fresh greenstuff will depend on whether they are browsing and foraging for themselves during the day, and the quality of the food they can get for themselves, in which case you will have to do very little of their work for them. However, if you are keeping them intensively you will have to bring green food to them as and when you can. Most greengrocers have more waste than they know what to do with and are pleased to let you have it. Pick it over carefully in case there is a plastic bag or any other dangerous item in it. It does not matter if the cauliflower trimmings are wilted and yellow, your goats will still enjoy them.

Hay and greens can be fed freely, though it is wise to make sure that hay has been eaten before anything lush is offered. Concentrates are fed at the morning and evening feeds, and for the milker you would give possibly half a pound of concentrates for body maintenance, and four ounces for each pint of milk given, divided between the two feeds. So a goat giving five pints of milk a day would be given fourteen ounces of concentrates each feed. Unfortunately, there are no set rules for feeding amounts, because goat systems and food quality vary so much, so the amounts given here are merely a guide. Be advised by the person who sells you your goats; if the animals are flourishing then they are being properly fed.

They will also need access to minerals. If there is any mineral deficiency in the diet the goat instinctively recognizes it and is able to compensate if you provide her with a mineral lick. Most goat-keepers also provide a cobalt or 'blue' block.

GROOMING AND FOOT CARE

Goats adore being groomed, tickled and fussed over. However, they are not so keen on having a pedicure, but it must be done, preferably once a month. The horny part of the hoof will grow over the sole if not attended to, and can encourage foot rot. This must be trimmed back with special shears sold as foot-rot shears. A sharp pruning knife can be used, and possibly gives better results, but one needs confidence and ability to use it. Less courage is needed to use the shears. One of the advantages of belonging to a goat club is the regular demonstrations there are of those essential tasks which can daunt the novice, such as hoof-trimming, drenching and worming.

MILKING

There are detailed instructions on how to do this in many of the books on goats. Practice on an old rubber glove filled with water is often recommended, but the best way is to be shown by some long-suffering goat-keeper on a patient goat who won't object too much when you take a turn. The very best way is to be forced into it. If you have a goat with a kid who will finish the job for you should you fail at first, you will very soon master the process, though at first your hands and forearms will be very tired.

One of the essentials of milking is to maintain the highest possible standard of hygiene. This means that all utensils must be sterilized with a dairy detergent, and kept in a clean place. Milk must be strained and cooled quickly under running water. Milk filters are available, fitting into a specially-made metal strainer. The metal strainer is expensive, and the funnel at the base rarely

A Jersey cow.

Traditional butter-making in South Uist.

Skimming off the cream from the cream pans with a scallop shell.

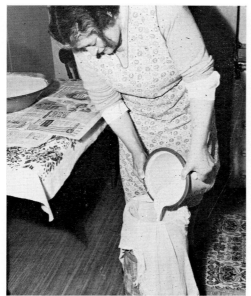
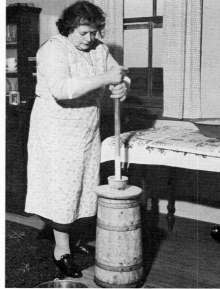

Pouring the cream through muslin into a wooden churn.

rning the butter when it is almost ready.

The butter being transferred into the salting pan.

hing out the buttermilk.

The finished product.

Young pigs can be kept
out of doors . . .
But they like to be kept
warm.

fits into any churn or jug you can buy. The simplest method, if you are not selling the milk commercially, is to buy a nylon sieve into which you can lay the filter, and pour the milk carefully through this.

HEALTH

With good care and management the vet need rarely be troubled, even at kidding time. However, if your goat consistently refuses her food, and stands about in a dejected manner, if the droppings are loose, or the milk yield drops dramatically, it is as well to seek professional advice. Often an experienced goat-keeper will sort you out, or help you to decide whether or not to call the vet.

By the time your goat is due to kid you will have learned to look for signs indicating difficulties. Remember that the goat is generally a healthy animal, and difficulty in kidding is the exception and not the rule, though one must always be prepared for anything.

COST

The cost of keeping a productive goat is difficult to arrive at since the price of foodstuff is continually increasing. One year hay can cost 25p a bale, the next £1.50. The easiest way to arrive at a rough budget is to estimate what your needs will be and balance this against local prices. There are special crops you can grow, if you have room left in your garden, and if you really mean business there is a considerable amount of wild food you can collect and feed green or dried. For the price of a bagging hook there are verges and patches of wild ground you can cut for hay. Your aim must be to make the whole venture as economical as possible. When you can pay for most of your hay and concentrates from the proceeds of the sale of goat produce to friends, bearing in mind the saving on household milk bills, then you can consider yourself successful.

Wild food

Ash, willow, hazel, brambles, holly, gorse, elm, oak, ivy, docks, thistles, nettles.

Poisonous plants

Rhododendron, yew, clematis, laburnum, laurel, ragwort, ivy berries.

Garden crops

Kale (thousand-headed), comfrey, lucerne, sainfoin; these are crops which can be specially grown. The goat will eat all the pea and bean haulms, and all the seasonal remains of the brassica crops from the garden.

Books
   Goats (Pet and Fancy Series, No. 8), H. C. Jeffrey, Cassell.
   Goat Keeping (Young Farmers Club booklet No. 8), Evans Brothers.
   Goat Husbandry, D. Mackenzie, Faber and Faber.

Breeds of goats
Breeds of goats found in the British Isles are: the British Alpine, the Toggenburg, the British Toggenburg, the Saanen, the British Saanen, the Anglo-Nubian and the Golden Guernsey. Full descriptions of these and their history can be found in specialist books.

Recipes

GOAT CHEESE
Keep milk for cheese-making as clean as possible. All utensils, bowls, etc., should be well scrubbed and boiled or rinsed out with boiling water. The milk should be cooled immediately after milking, as quickly as possible, before cheese-making starts. Do not use soap on any cloths; these should be washed in cold water, then in hot, and then boiled.

Lactic method
Buy a bottle of lactic acid from the chemists; it will probably have to be ordered for you, so it will be necessary to think ahead and get it in. It is unfortunately rather expensive, but it keeps indefinitely.
   Warm the milk to blood heat and pour it into a container which can be china, glass or plastic, but not metal. Add one teaspoon of lactic acid to each pint of the milk. The milk will curdle immediately, but should be left standing for twenty-four hours.
   Tip the curd through a large perforated strainer lined with muslin (a large steamer is perfect for the purpose) and leave it to drain for a further twenty-four hours.
   The curd can now be salted to taste and flavoured in any way that appeals to those who are going to eat it – with crushed garlic (or powdered garlic for a less strong flavour), chopped chives

and mixed fresh herbs such as parsley, mint and tarragon. It can be used in its unflavoured state to make cheesecake, or it can be frozen in plastic bags, just as it is, and salted and flavoured when required.

Natural souring

This gives a rather rougher texture and cheesier taste than the lactic method. Cool the milk as before and heat it to blood heat; it can then be left to sour with a dash of vinegar or half a lemon to help the souring process along. Proceed as for the lactic method.

KID

The meat of the kids is regarded as a gourmet's delight in France. Goat owners there are besieged by anxious cooks, who order their kid many months in advance and then wait on tenter-hooks to hear whether the kid is male, or female, in which case it will probably be kept for milk.

As kid is not likely to come the way of most people very often, a plainly roasted joint would probably be the first choice for the leg. Roast as for lamb, allowing 20 minutes per lb./450 g., with slivers of garlic and spiky leaves of rosemary inserted into the meat along the bone.

Kid can also be braised in a piece. Melt some butter in a heavy casserole, add two rashers of bacon, chopped onion, turnip, carrot and celery. Let this cook gently while you brown the meat on all sides in a mixture of butter and oil in the frying pan. Lay the browned meat on top of the vegetables and add a glass of cider, a small tin of tomatoes, thyme, marjoram, a crushed clove of garlic, salt and pepper. Cover and cook very gently until tender (2 to 4 hours, according to the size of the joint), then carve the meat and keep hot. Let the sauce boil and reduce until it is thick enough to coat the meat nicely, adjust the seasoning and serve.

CHAPTER FOUR

The House Cow

THE ADVANTAGES and the disadvantages of owning a
house cow are easy to perceive. An animal that must be milked
twice a day throughout the year is an additional responsibility
and a great tie. On the other hand, the value of fresh milk, cream
and butter throughout the year is very great. In the end I would
only commend the house cow to those who have a real affection
and affinity for animals. Cows, and especially Jersey cows, are
gentle and affectionate creatures. They respond to patient and
quiet handling. They are an ornament to any pasture and their
calves have the beauty of young deer.

For what follows I am indebted to Matthew Thorpe, who
provides practical advice based, as he says, on much trial and
frequent error. It is not so much for those who are wondering
whether or not to venture but for those who have decided to
take the plunge.

How to start

The land (see also Chapter 9, Using the grass from the garden)
A single animal of a small breed may be kept comfortably on
a piece of pasture of about two acres. That area should conveniently be divided into three paddocks. The land can then be

grazed and mown in rotation. Assuming that the venture is launched on old pasture in reasonable condition, not a great deal of attention to the land should be required to maintain it in good heart. A general fertilizer such as a 20:10:10 might be applied annually (see pages 129, 132). The supplier will generally arrange a contractor to spread it at small additional cost. The piece planned for mowing might be given a nitrogen dressing approximately six weeks before mowing in order to increase yield. The whole should be harrowed in the late autumn. In almost all areas contractors can be found to carry out all these operations involving machinery. Generally they will be found to be reliable, although hay-making that depends on contractors is always an even more anxious and less certain operation than usual (see pages 133–5 for hay-making). It is important to keep the pasture free of weed. If weeds are established or appear to spread the land should be sprayed in the spring with a general weed killer such as N.C.P. If a single weed species appears in isolated outbreaks then spot spraying with a specific poison applied through a knapsack spray is extremely effective.

Fencing

For different kinds of fencing, see the relevant section in Chapter 2 on sheep, and the illustrations on pages 130–1.

The animals

It is best to keep two house cows. Cows are naturally gregarious and prefer to be in the company of at least one other. Furthermore, if true independence of commercial milk is desired two cows are essential to ensure that at least one is in milk throughout the year. However, shortage of space would make it difficult for most people to keep more than one. The most suitable breeds for a house dairy cow are the Channel Island breeds. Perhaps best of all is the Jersey. Its virtues are well known: a small animal, extremely pretty, gentle-natured and easy to handle, economic in its grazing and rich in the quality of its milk. Its only disadvantage is its relatively low yield but that is a consideration which will not deter those who are not milking commercially. Other breeds that might be considered are, of course, the Guernsey and also the dairy shorthorn. The purchase of the milking cows is best left to a reliable dealer. He may buy at market or from an established herd. In either event his profit is an excellent insurance against the risk of a bad buy. The order should be for a cow in first lactation and she might well serve for as long as fifteen years if carefully looked after. It is therefore particularly important to buy well rather than cheaply. Points to look out for are: first, the udder, which should be firm, shapely and of average size, with well-placed teats and no supernumerary teats; second, the feet – the cow should look comfortable on her feet, straight-legged, not tending to walk on her heels.

Buildings

An out building of some description is essential. Although cows will winter out it is wise to keep them in at night in the winter unless the weather is mild. It is also convenient to bring a cow in for calving. Ideally, therefore, there will be a decent stall available. It should adjoin the milking area for convenience. The quality of the building is of little importance. As long as it is proof against the weather and has concrete floors, the absence of drainage will not matter. Nor need the milking parlours be any more sophisticated. A good concrete floor for washing down after each milking is the most important feature. A metal stall to hold the cow during milking and a built-in manger are con-venient but by no means essential. The buildings must also pro-vide storage for food and bedding. Bagged food will be bought in relatively small quantities and a galvanized corn bin of approxi-mately four cwt capacity can if necessary be stood up on a brick base in the milking parlour. The bin can be bought second-hand at a farm sale for an outlay that will quickly be recovered in the protection that it gives from rats and mice. However, the year's supply of hay and straw must be laid in between June and August, and dry storage is essential. There must be room for at least 50 bales overall, or 100 if two cows are kept, and if there happens to be a loft over the stalls and parlour there is no more convenient arrangement. It is also possible, though less satis-factory, to keep bales under a tarpaulin.

MANAGEMENT

Milking

The enthusiast who milks by hand is unlikely to resist the convenience of a machine indefinitely. A single-unit machine can be bought second-hand for about £50 including installation. It is well worth while to commission a dairy-equipment contractor to pick up a suitable machine and install it. He will generally know where a machine is to be found in the local farming community and he will know what is a fair price. The cow should be milked out from the first day of calving. The calf will not take all the yield, and unless milked the bag will become distended. For the first four days after calving the surplus is not fit for use and must be discarded. Thereafter, the cow must be milked twice a day until the end of lactation. The length of the lactation will depend on her next mating and the quality of the grass in each season. But as a general rule the cow could be dried off approximately eight weeks before the birth of the following calf. It is, therefore, important where two cows are being milked to establish calving cycles that will ensure that one cow is in full milk throughout the year. Drying off presents no problem. It may well happen naturally and if it does it should be accepted, even if premature. Otherwise, it can be achieved by reducing milking to once a day and then once every other day until the yield falls to nothing.

If a machine is used there is no essential need to strain the milk, but the machine must be thoroughly rinsed after ending milking. A bucket of cold water and a bucket of hot, sprinkled with dairy washing disinfectant, should be set beside the unit. Half the cold water should then be drawn through the machine, followed by all the hot water and finally the remainder of the cold. That simple operation takes only a few moments. At least once a month all parts of the unit that come in contact with milk must be stripped down and thoroughly cleaned with the disinfectant. A set of brushes designed to fit each diameter of pipe can be obtained from any supplier of dairy equipment. There are local firms, calling themselves suppliers of dairy sundries; ask any dairy farmer for the address of two or three of these, and then shop around, as prices vary widely.

The milk

Yield will vary greatly depending on the lactation cycles of the cows and the season of the year, but invariably there will be more than all but the largest households require. Since the quality of the milk is so rich there is much to be said for taking the cream from the entire yield and using skim as milk for all purposes. Whereas complete separation can only be achieved by the use of a small dairy separator, a satisfactory compromise is to stand the milk in bowls for twelve to twenty-four hours in the refrigerator or a cool larder and then to remove the cream with a pierced skimmer. Small separators are no longer made but are still reasonably easy to acquire second-hand. The electric separator is certainly much less effort than the manual but requires careful washing after each use. Since there are approximately forty separate parts to be stripped, washed and re-assembled the slightly superior result seems hardly worth the effort. The cream, however separated, can be used as it is or a proportion can be

Pan for setting cream

made into butter. The latter operation is relatively simple provided there is an electric butter churn of some description in the house. If any difficulty is encountered in procuring a churn then I have heard that an electric kitchen mixer can be adapted to do the work. The most convenient system is to make butter regularly once a week, putting surplus cream aside in the refrigerator through the intervening days. However, the cream must be stood in a warm room for several hours before it is poured into the churn. Chilled cream will not make butter no matter how long it is beaten. Nor will fresh skimmed cream make butter. Indeed, it is helpful if at least part of the cream to be used is on the turn.

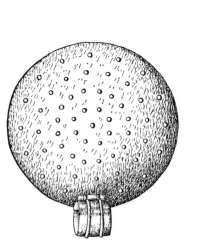
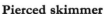

Pierced skimmer   **Butter churn**

Salt can be added to the cream if desired. Once the cream turns to butter it has only to be strained from the buttermilk and moulded into pats. (The method is given on pages 85–6.) Because of the absence of preservatives the life of home-made butter is short, but it can be stored very satisfactorily in a deep freeze until wanted. Buttermilk and any surplus skim makes excellent feed for a pig and there is much to be said for keeping a sow or fattening a couple of weaners at next to no cost with the surplus from the dairy. Alternatively cheese or yoghurt can be made at home in addition to cream and butter. Instructions on how to make yoghurt are included at the end of this chapter; see the goat chapter for making cheese.

Feed and health

The better a cow is fed the better she will yield. Although between May and September the cow will manage perfectly well on summer grass alone, it is advisable to give a bucket of dairy nuts at each milking. Cows are invariably greedy for concentrates and these milking feeds will bring them from the pasture to the machines at a shout, and will keep them quiet during milking. The additive to the feed prevents staggers and during July and August, when the protein value of the grass falls, the nuts will maintain the milk yield. During the winter the quantities should be increased. The diet can be varied by mixing in any or all of the following feeds: bran, crushed oats, flaked maize and molassed beet pulp, a by-product of sugar from sugar beet. The first is an almost essential ingredient of a balanced diet; the third is expensive, and thus a luxury, but is a favourite with the cow and can be used sparingly; the fourth is the cheapest bulk additive to the feed, but should be soaked for twelve hours before use since it is sold in a dehydrated state. In addition, whenever the cow is in the stall hay should be provided without stint. Whilst it is possible to feed barley straw to cattle, it is not to be recommended for a house cow in milk.

Straw for bedding in the stall should be wheat straw, which will always be cheaper to buy than barley straw. Cows can be deep-littered (on the same principle as chickens, see page 28) and if the droppings are removed daily the box need not be thoroughly mucked out more than about once a fortnight. The resulting manure is of obvious use in the garden.

Cows, particularly when only one or two animals are kept, are in the main remarkably free from disease or ailments. Mastitis, a painful and serious infection of the udder, is perhaps the commonest complaint and reveals itself at once in the milk, which will

F

appear pink in the pail. Mastitis should always be treated by the vet, for it can do permanent damage to the animal. Provided the cow is thoroughly stripped of her milk at each milking it should not occur in ordinary circumstances. It is as well to ensure that any cow bought in is free from tuberculosis and brucellosis. Although it is possible to join the brucellosis incentive scheme, owners of house cows will no doubt find it simpler to arrange for their vet to carry out an annual test as a precaution. The only other regular steps that should be taken to ensure that the cow remains in good health are to rub the teats with udder cream after each milking and to apply a fly repellent to the back and flanks of the animal during high summer. It may also be necessary to rub in a sprinkling of lice powder in the spring, when the cow is changing her coat. Signs of ill-health would be a sudden drop in the milk supply, loss of appetite, a 'stary' coat; get expert advice at once if anything seems to be wrong.

Calves and calving

In order to maintain a milk yield it is, as everyone knows, necessary that a cow should be kept calving. Service presents no problem. As soon as a cow shows sign of heat the local artificial insemination station should be telephoned and the type of semen required, should be ordered. The call will invariably be answered the next day and the cow will be inseminated without trouble and at a modest charge. It is easy enough to tell a cow's heat. She will rush about the field as though desperate to escape, particularly if other cattle are in the vicinity. She will not settle anywhere and will low constantly. The cow may be served on any heat after the last calving but the heat approximately sixty days after the last calving is the most fertile. If she does not take at the first service she should be served again at each heat until she conceives. If she has difficulty in getting into calf, the cause is very probably a mineral deficiency, and expert advice should be obtained. However, the need for repeat services on a healthy cow are rare. The choice of semen is wide. There is much to be said for breeding pedigree stock and no result is more successful than if a heifer calf is produced. But a Jersey bull calf is useless and valueless and there is therefore much advantage in a beef cross, particularly if there is no desire to breed a replacement or addition to the milking cow. Of the beef crosses the Charollais is among the most successful but some regard must be had for the cow before a Charollais cross is attempted. The calves tend to be large and so a Charollais cross should *not* be put on a cow calving for the first or second time, or on a particularly small cow.

Calving itself should present no great difficulty. Although cows can perfectly well be left to calve in the field, it is probably safer to bring a house cow in for the last few days before calving. In ninety-nine cases out of a hundred your cow will calve naturally and unaided. But she must be watched against that one per cent risk of difficulty. If the cow seems to be in heavy labour for several hours without result it is wise to call the vet. For it usually means that the calf is upside down or the wrong way round, and although an experienced dairyman will manage all but the most difficult deliveries the amateur will always be wise to pay a vet's bill rather than risk losing cow and calf.

After birth the calf should be allowed to suckle for at least five days. Thereafter the sooner it is weaned the easier the operation will be for the cow. On the other hand the calf will do exceptionally well if left on the cow for two or three weeks from birth. After that it must be weaned whether it is destined for market or for rearing. If it is intended for market it should be sent within the first three weeks, although the bigger and stronger it appears the more it will make. If it is intended for rearing it should be started on milk-powder bucket feed as soon as it is taken from the cow. Some days of patience will be needed to teach it to drink from the bucket unaided but, once it has learnt, rearing is little trouble. Calves will suck at anything, so put your finger in the calf's mouth and, as it starts to suck vigorously, bring down your hand into the milk bucket. The calf will then suck up the milk. You may have to leave your fingers in its mouth while it feeds, until it gets the hang of it. Calf pellets and hay should be put out almost from the start and you will be surprised how quickly the calf learns to eat solids.

If the calf is to be sold a local haulage contractor will collect for market and make all necessary arrangement at the market itself. The market will then settle by cheque within a relatively short time, deducting its charge from the gross sale price. Whilst it is perfectly possible to keep and rear a beef cross bull calf it is probably wiser to sell at the two/three-week stage. Under no circumstances would it be wise to raise a pedigree Jersey bull calf. If the cross-bred bull calf is to be raised for beef the vet will arrange castration and de-horning and will advise on any current beef subsidy scheme.

The economics

In making elementary calculations, it must be assumed that necessary pasture and outbuildings are available and can be brought into the account at no cost. Thereafter, the value of the home dairy depends in part on the size of the household and the amount previously spent on commercial dairy produce. Equally, it is hard to bring labour into the account at any precise figure. Milking and all the other jobs that are necessary to get the most from a house cow are enjoyable and not particularly time-consuming, but they are a great tie and I would not advise anyone to embark on a house cow unless there is someone available to take their fair share of the work, if only on a relief or occasional basis.

Leaving these elements out of account, the capital items are:

  1 cow
  1 milking machine
  1 butter churn
  Bins, buckets, brushes and other incidentals

The cost of all these items should be assessed after discussion locally; the same applies to running costs. Prices vary widely in different areas and inflation must also be taken into account.

The annual items of expenditure are:

  $\frac{1}{2}$ ton hay at cost to make
  $\frac{1}{2}$ ton straw bought in
  $\frac{1}{2}$ ton mixed bagged food
  1 gallon washing disinfectant
  1 gallon udder cream
  Vet's bill

The benefits per cow are:

  Average daily yield throughout year – 2 gallons
  1 calf per annum
  1 ton of garden manure

It would be wise, before embarking, to cost out all these items very carefully on the basis of local, up-to-date information. But the real justification is the pleasure that the cow will give when healthy and in full milk, and the satisfaction of a constant supply of dairy products that have not been pasteurized, homogenized or adulterated.

Recipes

YOGHURT

Yoghurt can easily be made at home without any special equipment or skills; this is not surprising when you consider that it is made all over the world in all sorts of temperatures and often primitive conditions.

Ordinary commercial yoghurt contains the live organisms that turn milk into yoghurt. There is no need to buy 'live' yoghurt to use as a starter, but any yoghurt used should be as fresh as possible.

Boil 2 pints (1·2 litres) of fresh milk and leave it in a covered china or glass dish to cool until it is a little warmer than blood heat (46 °C/115 °F is the recommended heat). Whisk in 2 table-spoons of yoghurt, cover with cling-wrap and keep it warm until the yoghurt sets, which will take about three or four hours.

People use various methods for keeping the yoghurt warm while it is making. I put mine on the bread board and stand it on the back of the Aga; I have also made yoghurt in the airing cup-board wrapped in a blanket. My sister makes her yoghurt in her electric oven, turned to its lowest possible heat. You can buy an electric yoghurt-making machine, which keeps the incubating yoghurt at exactly the best temperature, but with a bit of experi-menting it should be possible to make perfectly satisfactory yoghurt without going to such lengths.

After cooling, the yoghurt is best refrigerated for a few hours, still covered with cling wrap, or it may pick up unwanted tastes from the refrigerator. As the yoghurt chills, it thickens and be-becomes more creamy. It will keep for several days in the refri-gerator, but is best made and eaten daily. Use some of it as a starter for the next making.

Sometimes other organisms invade the yoghurt and you will have to start again with another pot of commercial yoghurt as a starter. Sometimes the yoghurt 'weakens'; the incubation period becomes longer or the yoghurt may not set at all and it will be necessary to buy yoghurt to get going again. But most of the time everything goes like clockwork and there will be bowls of lovely fresh yoghurt, to eat as it is or to use in cooking or salads as a delicious and healthy alternative to cream.

CHEESE

Cow's milk cheese can be made in the same manner as goat's milk cheese (see page 74).

BUTTER MAKING

Butter is made once or twice a week from the cream that has been skimmed each day from milk which has been put to stand in wide shallow bowls for 12 to 24 hours. A proper skimmer can be used, or a substitute such as a scallop shell. Skimming will not remove all the cream, so the skim milk can be used for drinking and kitchen purposes.

Before churning, the cream must stand in a warm room for

several hours until it reaches a temperature of between 56 °F and 62 °F. As Matthew Thorpe says, cream for churning should not be too fresh (see page 80). Small quantities can be churned in an electric mixer, set to the lowest possible speed. Continue the slow whisking until the cream first thickens, changes colour and then separates into grains of butter and thin buttermilk. When the whole bowlful has separated, drain in a fine sieve, stir until the butter grains start to coalesce and drain again. Add cold water to the butter, swish it around and strain again, repeating this process three times. Drain thoroughly, then put the butter on a clean board, sprinkle it with salt (about one teaspoonful per pound), and knead it thoroughly to remove the last traces of buttermilk. Then pat it into shape.

If butter is to be made frequently it would be worth acquiring an electric churn. There are various types on the market and they are sold with instructions for their use. After the butter has formed in the churn, the process is completed as above. Home-made butter will not keep very long but it can be frozen and used as required, perhaps while the house cow is dry. As with all milk products, the utmost cleanliness is necessary when making butter.

A good source of ideas for what to do with milk products on a small scale is Maggie Black's paperback *Home-made Butter, Cheese and Yoghurt*, published by E.P. Publishing Ltd., 1977.

VEAL

Should you have an unwanted bull calf (or like me, have farming parents who are generous with their unwanted bull calves) you will have a lot of veal. Veal can be a rather boring meat; the texture is nice but the flavour has to be helped. The offal is the real treat. Calf's heart, which never seems to be on sale at the butcher's in the ordinary way, is excellent stuffed and then braised in a little stock. The liver is a delicacy and luckily calves seem to have very large livers. I like to cut the liver into the thinnest possible slices, coat them lightly with seasoned flour, fry them in butter until just done, one minute on each side should be enough, add a squeeze of lemon and a sprinkling of parsley and eat as soon as possible, with fried mushrooms and a green salad.

Veal is a good vehicle for other flavours; Gruyère cheese, Parmesan cheese, olives, tomatoes, anchovies, bacon, ham, garlic, capers, gherkins, lemons, oranges, sorrel are used in various recipes to give flavour, while bacon fat, butter, eggs, cream or sour cream can be used to counteract the dryness of the meat.

Veal cutlets on the bone, trimmed, can be dipped in beaten egg and then into seasoned breadcrumbs and fried in butter until crisp. A variation is to add freshly grated Parmesan cheese to the seasoned breadcrumbs.

Another method is to fry the cutlets gently in butter, then place in a dish sandwiched between layers of chopped sautéd onion, add a glass of wine, red or white, and a cup of stock, season and cover with a layer of fresh breadcrumbs and grated Parmesan cheese. Cook in a hot oven (450 °F/230 °C/gas mark 8) until the top is brown and crisp.

Escalopes are usually flattened by beating with a rolling pin, egged, breadcrumbed, and fried, in the way described for cutlets, and served with slices of lemon and sprigs of parsley. It is fatally easy to let them get soggy. Clarified butter is the best fat to fry them in, or a mixture of oil and butter, and they should be eaten the minute they are done.

If you can't cook and eat them in the kitchen, straight from the pan, try another way. When I lived for a while in Rome I was fond of eating saltimbocca, which means 'jump into the mouth' – a tribute to the deliciousness of the dish. The meat is cut and beaten into small thin slices and each piece is covered with a piece of lemon and fresh sage, then rolled up and skewered with a cocktail stick and fried in butter. Add a glass of wine, let it bubble and reduce and then cover the pan for a few minutes, leaving it on a very low heat so that the flavours can permeate the meat.

Escalopes are also very good with tomato purée. Flour and fry the meat in butter for a minute on each side, then add a mixture of sautéd finely chopped onions, skimmed and chopped tomatoes, fresh basil, salt and pepper; leave this cooking very gently until the sauce is syrupy, spooning it over the meat from time to time.

Roast veal is good boned and stuffed with sautéd onions, chopped walnuts, dried apricots soaked and then chopped, half a tin of anchovies, mashed with a fork, and grated lemon rind mixed with fresh breadcrumbs and bound with a beaten egg. Push the stuffing into the cavity where the bone was and sew it up with needle and thread. Roast in a moderate oven, (350°F/180°C/gas mark 4) allowing 30 minutes per lb./450 g. When dishing up, remove the thread from the meat and enrich the juices with cream.

CHAPTER FIVE

Pigs

HERE IS information strictly for the enthusiast, for pigs in the garden create quite a lot of problems. Housing and/or fencing must be really strong, for pigs are restless, intelligent and powerful animals. Our first two pigs, known as Strongy and Weaky, were confined in a fortress: an old-fashioned sty with a stout stone wall around the outdoor area and a stone and tiled shelter. There was a rather insanitary drain in the concrete floor of the pen and the shelter had no drainage. The arrangement was far from ideal, though picturesque in appearance, for the house with its brick floor was difficult to clean out and the job had to be done bending double, as the house was not high enough to stand upright in.

Pigs prefer to dung in one area, keeping the rest tolerably clean. In hot weather they are apt to reverse the usual process and dung inside their house, using the yard as their living area, which is disagreeable for you as their dung smells very strongly, and particularly in an enclosed area.

Smells and flies in the summer are concomitants of pigs in sties and must be added to the other disadvantages of pig-keeping: expensive housing, astronomical feed bills and the rather unpleasant task of mucking out. When considering keeping pigs you should also remember that they will have to be mucked out at least twice a week, and so you will need space for that rapidly increasing pile of pig manure where it will not annoy you or anyone else.

Financially the rewards of keeping pigs in sties are not great. I quote from a reader's letter in *Practical Self-Sufficiency*, a useful magazine published by Broad Leys Publishing Company, Widdington, Saffron Walden, Essex:

> I think readers would be interested to know the actual cost of pig-keeping and also that it is not possible to feed a pig on household scraps as it needs 3 lbs of food per day which no self-sufficient household worth its salt would create. Therefore pigs have to be fed on pig nuts or similar from a feed merchant (swill is illegal). I had 4 pigs on 30 October 1975.

4 pigs, 12 weeks old	£80.00
19 November – Pellets	9.99
11 December – Pig trough –	
they made a hole in the old one	6.50
18 December – Pellets (5 cwt)	24.23
16 January – Pellets (10 cwt)	45.95
2 February – carriage to market	2.50
	£169.17

Cost per pig £42.30

And that is without costing in the straw which is £20 per ton and they need 2–3 bales per week.

Here in Kent we have to pay considerably more for our straw, which bought in small quantities is 95p per bale. Should you live in a corn-growing area, it is infinitely cheaper to collect the straw yourself, buying it off the field. Food costs also have been rising steadily and any figures are speedily out of date, but I can state from experience that it is expensive.

However, if bought-in pigs are fattened on bought pig foods alone, the pork works out at about 25 per cent cheaper than bought meat; if clever use is made of the garden-farmer's own resources, the same pigs can be reared for about half the price of the meat in the shops. This is assuming that the pigs are kept warm, either in good housing or by propitious weather conditions, and assuming of course that there are no disasters such as disease. The cost of housing and labour is not taken into account either.

How to start

The first thing is to decide on the scope of your operation. The choices are:

1 To buy one little weaner and fatten it up to a porker.
2 To buy two or more weaners and fatten them up to porkers.
3 To keep on one or more porkers to become baconers.
4 To breed your own piglets up to weaners and then keep as
   many as you require, selling the rest.

I am assuming that most people who want to keep pigs in their
gardens, with all that this implies, will be primarily interested in
buying weaners and fattening them, finding the idea of keeping a
sow and breeding from her rather too elaborate. So this chapter
will deal with keeping and fattening bought-in weaners.

Think out the housing and/or fencing, remembering that while
fresh air and exercise out of doors are very good for sows and
piglets, fattening pigs must be kept indoors and sows must be
brought in to have their litters.

Buying weaners

Pig farmers, who have to think of their overheads, rear pigs in
insulated housing all the year round, but the garden-farmer will
probably only require one or two pigs a year and therefore these
should be reared in the summer, when housing need not be of
such a high standard as the weather will save those valuable
calories. On the other hand, most people think of pork as a winter
meat. So the ideal time to buy the weaners would be early July for
slaughtering at the end of September; then the meat should last
you through to March.

A local farmer might well be prepared to buy weaners for you,
taking a cut on the deal, obviously. He would probably be happy
to transport the little pigs to you. It is necessary to have a licence
for the movement of pigs, a precaution against disease. The pig
dealer will give you the filled-in form.

If you have no farmer friend to help you, contact a local pig-
dealer. There should be a list in the yellow pages of the local
telephone directory; if possible make some personal enquiries.
The ideal age for weaners is from eight to ten weeks old, this
being the time that the piglets become independent of their
mother, and as you will be paying for them by weight it is a good
thing to buy them as young and small as possible.

I strongly recommend buying a minimum of two little pigs, for
pigs are happier and warmer when reared together. It might be
possible to share the pigs with another family. We, as a family of
five (two adults, three children), find it quite easy to get through
two porkers, but our circumstances are perhaps unusual in that
my husband works at home, so we often have people to feed at

lunchtime as well as friends who come to spend weekends with us in the country and need plenty of good food to help them to endure our icy home. Pork does not have a very long life in the freezer and I should have thought that one porker would do a normal family very nicely.

Many cottages in former times used to keep one pig. Often the poorest families could only buy the runt of the litter and with the care that was lavished on it the little pig often thrived extremely well, but one pig will always need more attention, companionship from humans and closer care of its warmth and comfort.

If possible, choose the piglets yourself. You do not need to be an expert to pick out the ones that are most lively and thrust their way through their siblings to get the best of whatever is going. It is rather like choosing a puppy.

Housing

Pigs have no fur and they need warm, dry housing if they are to do well. When they go to bed they burrow into their straw, pulling it over themselves like an eiderdown, and they also cuddle together for warmth. On the other hand they cannot bear to be too hot and in the summer of 1976 I used to give our pigs showers and baths in the middle of the day, to their great delight. A well-insulated house is essential therefore, cool in summer and warm in winter. It should face south. The housing also should be as easy to clean as possible and it should be strong, as pigs are destructive animals.

Building a house

The house should be big enough to allow the pigs to sleep there in comfort when grown. Six feet by four feet would make two porkers very comfortable. The yard should be rather bigger, six feet by six feet, to allow room for the troughs. The floor of the house must (I write with some feeling) be raised above the floor level of the yard, and sloping into it for good drainage. This is absolutely essential. It would be a good thing to have ventilation shutters under the roof and, if you are going to keep pigs during cold weather, swing doors to keep the house warm. It would be useful to have a bolt on the door, so that you can sweep out the yard without being bothered by playful pigs.

If the house is to be made of wood, it is a good idea to cover the inside walls with corrugated iron to discourage the pigs from chewing them.

The roof should be well insulated. Asbestos sheeting is better than corrugated iron, which is very cold in winter and hot in

summer. If corrugated iron is to be used it should be well insulated, for otherwise much expensive pig food will be wasted
in keeping the animals warm. Do-it-yourself shops provide rolls
of insulating material which is effective and easy to use. A sky-
light would give light, which is good for the pigs and makes
cleaning easier.

The house should be high enough, at least at one point, to
allow a man to stand upright, otherwise cleaning out is agonizing.

The yard should ideally be surrounded by a strong wall of
brick, stone, breeze blocks or timber. The door should not be
opposite the door of the house or there will be draughts, which
pigs do not like any more than we would. It should slope to an
efficient drain.

Detailed design must depend on the site and your requirements,
but if the above points are kept in mind, it will not be difficult to
design or adapt some suitable building.

You will need a dry place to keep the necessary straw.

A stand-pipe near the sty with a hosepipe is useful for sluicing
down the floors after cleaning out. A watertight rat-proof container for the food, such as a second-hand zinc feed bin or a dust-
bin with a well-fitting lid, a scoop, troughs for food and for
water, a shovel and a broom complete the equipment. I also keep
bleach or disinfectant to pour down the drain occasionally and an
aerosol animal insecticide to discourage flies and other pests; I
find that I need to use this every two or three days when flies are
troublesome, or the pigs become most uncomfortable.

MANAGEMENT

Water

Either check that there is water in the troughs at least three
times a day, or install an automatic water supply. Pigs often knock
over their troughs and can then suffer from thirst.

Feeding

The modern pig has been bred to grow fast on concentrated
food and enterprising British pig producers export their stock all
over the world.

So, if you want a pig that will grow quickly without putting on
too much fat, and you cannot spare very much time, I would recommend buying weaners from a reputable dealer and feeding
them entirely on pig nuts which you can buy from a corn merchant. Bear in mind that animals fed on dry foods need to drink
a lot of water. The manufacturers of the nuts provide useful

feeding charts, but a good rule of thumb is a quarter of a pound per day for every week of the pig's age. Thus, allow 2 lb. per day for a weaner of 8 weeks old, 2½ lb. per day when it is 10 weeks old and so on.

This varies slightly according to the type of food used and the best thing is to follow the maker's chart. A typical guide is as follows, allowing extra in cold weather:

Age	approx. weight of pig (lb.)	lb. of food pellets per day		lb. per week
8 weeks	40	2·0	high-protein pig-growing pellets	14·0
9 weeks	49	2·3		16·1
10 weeks	59	3·0		21·0
11 weeks	69	3·3		23·1
12 weeks	80	3·8	start change to fast-growing pellets	26·6
13 weeks	91	3·7		25·9
14 weeks	100	3·85		26·95
15 weeks	109	4·0		28·0
16 weeks	118	4·15		29·05
17 weeks	127	4·25		29·95
18 weeks	136	4·4		30·8
19 weeks	145	4·6		32·2

Total   303·65 lb.

or roughly 2¾ cwt.

To take a pig on to a heavy porker weight of about 200 lb. live weight will take more food, up to about 3½ cwt. in total. Some people ration the pigs to 4½ lb. per day when this daily amount has been reached.

Pigs, particularly the modern fast-growing breeds, are subject to digestive troubles, especially when they are young, so there is much to be said for using the well-tried, balanced, commercially produced pellet. This is the foolproof easy way of growing meat which will still be better and cheaper than anything you can buy in the shops.

When the weaners are bought, it is a good thing to inquire what feed they have been having and to continue with the same; any changeover should be made gradually until they are on their fast-growing pig pellets. They should be fed twice a day and should have plenty of fresh water available at all times. There should always be adequate trough space or the weakest will go without.

Feeding on home-produced foods

It is certainly possible to fatten pigs partly on home-grown foods, and especially if you can mix it with skim milk from your own cow. This method requires quite a lot of time and energy and I will not go into it except to make the following points and list foods commonly used.

1 If pigs are to be allowed out to forage and graze, they should be on 'clean' ground – that is, ground where pigs have not been kept during the last three years. Pigs are very subject to parasites; the eggs of the roundworms that attack pigs can remain in the soil for three years and they are not destroyed by drought or frost. The earthworms in the soil are hosts to a particularly unpleasant lung worm which attacks pigs. So grazing pigs need a lot of land, to be grazed in rotation.

2 Most people, however keen they may be on rearing pigs nature's way, bring them in for fattening. This is because pigs fatten best when kept warm and spared from all exertion. A pig, however hard he tries, grows tubby without exercise.

3 I do not think it is possible for anybody who does not work full-time on the plot to grow enough food for the pigs, particularly when he is trying to grow food for other animals as well.

4 If the food (such as potatoes) is to be boiled, this will involve you in a lot of boiling. Raw potatoes can be fed to pigs, but they are far less digestible and the pigs will not do as well as they will on boiled potatoes.

5 A pig's intestine is only half the length of that of a cow or sheep, in proportion to its size. This means that it cannot digest efficiently food which is very bulky or fibrous. In fact, a pig's digestive system is not unlike our own. Young pigs particularly cannot do well on such foods as potatoes, which are very bulky in proportion to their food value, or coarse greenstuff.

6 If greenstuff is to be fed to pigs in sties, take account of the fact that their droppings will be smellier, looser and more frequent.

Pigs' needs

Water, protein, carbohydrates, minerals, vitamins and roughage. The following lists may be helpful:

Pigs

Protein sources

skim milk	soya meal	fish and meat
meat meal	beans	scraps
fish meal	peas	

Carbohydrate sources

barley meal	wheat meal	potatoes
maize meal		

Mineral sources

cereals	fish meal	meat meal

Vitamin sources

root vegetables	sunlight	cod liver oil
fresh green food	fish meal	

Suitable green foods

grass	lucerne	cabbage
clover	comfrey	kale

Suitable root vegetables

potatoes	turnips	Jerusalem
carrots	swedes	artichokes

Foods which are harmful to pigs
very salty foods
anything containing detergent or washing soda
food which is frozen (this can be a danger when surplus food
  is left lying in troughs in frosty weather)
sour leftovers from previous meals
rhubarb leaves
potato haulms
tomato plants
peel of citrus fruits
any bad or rotting fruits
potatoes which have gone green through exposure to light

Litter
Straw is by far the best litter. Two pigs will need a bale per
week.

Disease
There are stringent precautions in force to prevent the spread
of pig disease, and pigs from a good dealer should arrive free

from disease and parasites. However, there are pig diseases which *must* be reported (see Chapter 12) and anyone who keeps pigs should call the vet at once if any pig looks diseased, off its food, shivery, or lame. Don't skimp on the vet's visits, for a pig is a valuable animal. I also feel that a porker's life, being so short, should be made as happy and comfortable as possible.

Slaughtering

I have a neighbour who slaughtered his pig himself; though he is good with his hands, strong and resourceful he said he would never do it again. Another friend told me, 'The worst part was de-hairing it. It took all morning to de-hair the back side of one small pig.'

We take ours to the butcher. It saves money to transport the pigs yourself. It is quite possible to take two porkers in a small estate car with a back seat that folds over. Wedge a roll of pig netting to stop the pigs from climbing into the front of the car, cover the floor of the back with straw, then find something to act as a ramp, such as a couple of stout planks, or an old door. Discourage the pigs from running out at the side of the ramp by placing the side of the car against a wall and improvising a 'wing' on the other side of the ramp. The pigs can then either be enticed up the ramp with a bucket of food, or manhandled up with an ear in each hand, which they resent keenly whilst it is going on but forget when they see all that lovely clean straw on the floor of the car back.

Two people are needed, or the first pig will try to come out while you are pushing the second pig in.

Recipes

Roast pork

To make the crackling really crackle and, at the same time, to get rid of a lot of the fat, rub the rind of the joint with olive oil and salt and put it into a hot oven for five to ten minutes. It will then be easy to score the fat deeply, making the cuts half an inch apart. The fat will melt as the joint cooks, leaving the crispy crackling and a thin layer of fat. Baste frequently and cook until the joint shrinks.

If the joint is to be eaten cold (and cold pork is particularly good) it is better to cook it slowly, with the rind removed. Start it off in a moderate oven (350 °F/180 °C/gas mark 4), seasoned with salt and pepper, garlic, rosemary or fennel, or stuck with cloves; after half an hour add a pint (6 dl.) of good stock to the roasting tin and cover the whole thing with foil. Leave to cook slowly and thoroughly, 30–40 minutes per lb. (450 g.). When cooked, either leave it to cool in the larder, still wrapped in foil and lying in its juices or take it out while hot, spread some honey over the joint and glaze it in a hot oven (450 °F/230 °C/gas mark 8) until brown and glistening.

Rillettes

Last summer, when we were just coping with the meat from two freshly killed pigs, we happened to have a French family staying with us. The mother of the family offered to make rillettes and they have now become a staple of our diet, being very easy to make, very good and popular with all age groups. You need:

Belly of pork	Black peppercorns
Bayleaves	Salt
Thyme	and a heavy pan with a lid

Cut the belly of pork into short strips. Put it into the pan with the bayleaves, thyme, black peppercorns, salt and freshly ground black pepper to taste. It must be highly seasoned.

Cover the pan. Let the meat sweat gently on the lowest possible heat for four or five hours, or until the meat is falling to pieces. Pour off the fat and juices into a bowl and set aside. Put the meat on a board and mash it up with a fork, removing any little bones or any pieces of skin which have failed to disintegrate.

Pack the meat into scrupulously clean jam jars or foil containers, seal the pots with ½ inch of the fat and cover with foil. Rillettes will keep for weeks in the larder or the refrigerator so long as the seal is not broken. Or they can be frozen.

One can experiment with various flavours for rillettes, such as garlic, juniper berries, nutmeg; the only thing which must not vary is the very slow cooking; this keeps the shreds of pork soft and juicy.

CURING

During the last war the Ministry of Agriculture put out instructions for the curing of pig meat, in order that the meat could be kept throughout the year and only the spare rib, blade bone, trimmings and offal eaten fresh; this was known as the Standard Graduated Cure. The idea was to kill the pig in cold weather – the temperature at killing time should be less than 50 °F

G

and the temperature of the curing room should be 40 °F. Close humid weather should be avoided.

The pig having been killed and bled, scraped and cut up correctly, a brine bath was prepared. 13 lb. of salt, 4 oz. of saltpetre was mixed with 5 gallons of hot water and allowed to cool completely. The joints were then immersed in this for anything up to one hour according to the thickness of the meat.

The meat was then removed from the brine and the actual curing process began. The recommended curing mixture was: 5 lb. dry salt and 2 oz. of saltpetre to 50 lb. of meat (i.e., the salt was one-tenth of the weight of the meat). Care was taken to see that the small quantity of saltpetre was thoroughly mixed with the salt.

The skin was rubbed very thoroughly with the curing mixture and the flesh rubbed more lightly. The thicker the joint, the more of the mixture was used. A large bench was covered with a 2-inch-thick layer of dry salt; the joints were pressed into this, skin side down and sprinkled with curing mixture. More salt was then packed around the joints and a further 2-inch layer of salt covered the whole.

Five days later the process was repeated, using fresh salt, and the cuts could from then on be removed at intervals according to the depth of cure required.

When the joints were removed, the salt was brushed off, the surface of the meat wiped dry with a cloth and the joints hung up in an airy place until dry. They were then wrapped in muslin or calico and hung up in a cool dry place, away from direct sunlight and flies.

The length of time that the joints were cured depended on the thickness of the meat and the length of time they were to be kept. In the days before freezers very little could be eaten fresh. The blade bone was roasted and the spare ribs used as chops, the offal and the tripe eaten fresh, the head made into brawn, and sausages made from the trimmings, black puddings from the blood and so on, but the bulk of the meat was cured.

A lightly cured piece spent 3 to 4 days in the salt per inch of thickness; it would then keep for a month or two.

A medium cure involved 5 to 6 days in the salt per inch of thickness; the meat would then keep for four months.

Well-cured meat spent anything between 6 and 10 days in the salt per inch of thickness, bacon receiving a stronger cure than ham, and would keep the whole year. No piece, however thick, was left in the salt for more than 5 weeks.

No sugar was used at this date; it was not available in wartime, but is now used to counteract the toughening action of the salt.

The above is reliable if not gastronomically exciting. For lots of ideas for short-term curing (and long-term, but with many warnings of possible failure) Jane Grigson's *Charcuterie and French Pork Cookery*, published by Penguin, is invaluable.

CHAPTER SIX

Bees

'When I started keeping bees I didn't have a sting for a whole year – and then it was because I knocked into the hive with the Flymo when I was wearing shorts and a T-shirt . . .'

SU GOODERS

WHY DO not more people keep bees? One person can look after at least one hundred hives and a reasonable harvest from each hive would be forty-five lb. of honey. Beekeeping is labour intensive – for the bees. The beekeeper, once experienced, has an easy and absorbing pastime.

Our beekeeping experience is short; we were encouraged into it by a friend, a Londoner, with a busy life and two children, who can only visit her bees at weekends when she is not travelling all over the world in her highly demanding full-time job. Her experiences have formed the basis for this chapter, for it was she who disposed of my two major doubts; am I brave enough? Have I the time?

You might find that you spend a lot of money on equipment only to find that you are allergic to bee stings. So the first thing to establish, for those who wish to keep bees, is that they can tolerate bee stings. Some people react very badly when stung; it may even be extremely dangerous for those people to incur any risk of bee stings. So join the local beekeepers' association and find someone who will allow you to handle his bees – and get stung.

It is also essential to have a real enthusiasm for watching and studying the bees. They are not remotely domesticated, even after the thousands of years in which man has looked after them. Bee-keeping now is arousing great interest; many suppliers are unable to cope with the sudden demand. But I wonder how many people will give up beekeeping because they started for purely financial reasons and have not the patience and interest to surmount the early difficulties.

The life of the colony

The beekeeper's role is largely that of an onlooker; sometimes he is called upon to forestall some natural disaster which might wipe out a colony of bees in the wild. He should be able to frustrate the bees' natural instinct to swarm; or to retrieve a swarm should it leave the hive. He will also feed the bees when this is necessary. But by and large his role is a passive one, for the bees will continue to preserve the life of the colony in so far as they are able to do this, and to make the quantities of honey which will provide them with their winter store. They make more honey than they will need, and it is this surplus which man has harvested since time immemorial.

The whole effort of a hive of bees is directed towards the survival of the colony from year to year, either intact or by making a breakaway swarm with the queen to start a new colony else-where, leaving the old hive with a skeleton quota of worker bees and a young unfertilized queen, who is yet to mate and start laying. It is this instinct to survive that makes the bees produce more honey than they need. They use the stores of honey and pollen to feed the larvae and themselves and for provisions for the winter. A successful hive is one that has a young and vigor-ously laying queen, and which can support enough worker bees through the winter to ensure a large band of foragers and nurse bees for the larvae in spring, when the yearly work begins again.

The individual bees are highly specialized. The queen's task is to mate and to lay eggs. The drones, born from unfertilized eggs, exist solely to fertilize the queen; they are thrown out to die at the end of the summer. The workers feed and tend the larvae, make wax for the combs, clean the hive, forage for nectar and honey, scout for new sources of food or suitable places for a swarm to nest, cool the hive when necessary by fanning their wings – in short, they are the proletariat. The whole life of a

colony is utterly fascinating and the successful beekeeper is one
with the patience and determination to work with the colony and
understand its ways. With understanding will come greater confidence and the calm precision which minimizes stings and suits
the bees, too.

How to start

Assuming that you are not allergic to bee stings and that there
is a suitable site for bees in your garden, the first step is to contact
the secretary of the local beekeeping association who will supply
the name and address of a bee dealer in your area. It is a good idea
to buy locally because follow-up visits are easy to arrange; the
dealer will have his reputation to think of and his bees will be
suitable to the area. Different bees thrive in different places. There
is no need to worry if your particular patch does not have exactly
the same vegetation or aspect as the dealer's, for bees forage over a
distance of two miles and they will find what suits them.

When contacting the bee dealer, make it clear that this is a new
venture and that you would like him to visit you once the bees
are installed to see that all is well.

Equipment

This must all be in apple-pie order before the bees are due to
arrive. Second-hand hives are a good bargain, but the last thing
you want is to have to try to mend them once the bees are inside;
far better to check them over thoroughly for anything even
slightly unsatisfactory. If the frames are not squared up so that
they do not drop in and out easily, or there is anything loose or
unsound, get a really competent carpenter or handyman to over-
haul the hives if, like us, you are not very skilful. They must be
thoroughly disinfected before use.

Types of hive

Those traditional, white-painted, weather-boarded hives are
known as W.B.C. hives. They are the best looking hives on the
market, but they have disadvantages. They are heavy. They are
expensive. They are not made in standard sizes, so spares are more
difficult to obtain. Their chief advantage, apart from their
appearance, is their insulation, but opinions differ on the importance of this and probably most amateur beekeepers starting now
would recommend the National hive, which is light, simple and
made in standard sizes. Only use one type of hive: this is essential,
or the shed will become littered with spares and equipment of
different sizes, which will never fit when needed.

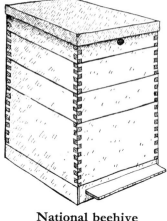
National beehive

WBC beehive

How many hives?

One hive would provide enough honey for the average family, but two would provide twice as much honey for very little more trouble. Two hives protect the beekeeper against the catastrophe of losing all his bees through some disaster; should one of the colonies be without a fertile queen, there is a handy free source for replacement (a Buckfast queen would cost you £5); should there be too much honey it is an easy matter to dispose of it at a very good price. Three hives would be better still; one could be left empty then to receive possible swarms. Optimists can try siting the empty hive under a tree, where a passing swarm might well find the tree, and later the hive, attractive.

Other equipment

The essential items are:

A smoker.

A hive tool, which is a kind of knife-cum-scraper and is absolutely indispensable.

A bee-veil and hat. This can be improvised with a stiff, wide-brimmed straw sun hat and a nylon net curtain dyed black. It must be black or the beekeeper cannot see clearly. Thread the curtain on to elastic which holds it firmly around the base of the crown of the hat – where the ribbon would have been. Allow enough netting to fall generously over the shoulders. Stitch in a curved piece of wire at about nose level to keep the veil away from the face. Make slits up the sides for the shoulders.

The best type of all, however, is the square cage-type veil with elastic around the neck; this can be bought from a dealer.

A bee suit. This can be bought, or again can be improvised out of a pair of workman's overalls with the buttons replaced by Velcro, which leaves no gaps. Tuck the trouser legs into socks and wear wellington boots.

Gloves. These should be special beekeeper's gloves made of thin leather; they are tight-fitting up the wrist and then come up to mid-forearm, covering the cuffs completely.

Canvas to cover the frames during inspections of the hives.

Siting the hives

People have been known to keep bees on their roofs in cities, but this is not ideal as roof tops are windy and cold. A better site would be in the garden, away from the house and areas where people sit or children play. Some sort of screen, such as bushes, a fence or hedge, in front of the hives is advisable, because it defines the territorial area in which the bees are likely to attack; it also helps to set the bees on a higher flight path where they are less likely to clash with people. The screen should not be too near the hives or the bees, which home by sight, may be confused.

If the hives are tilted slightly forward this protects the entrance from rain. They should be raised on bricks to discourage mice, which can be a disaster.

The grass just in front of the hives should be kept short. Weedkiller could be used safely in the winter when the bees are not active but it is better to clip the grass occasionally with shears.

MANAGEMENT

May would be a good month to start, so February/March could be spent accumulating equipment and contacting the bee dealer well in advance.

The hives are divided into two main sections. At the bottom of the hive are the brood chambers, where the queen lays her eggs in cells to provide workers, drones and replacement queens. Next comes the 'queen excluder', made of mesh coarse enough to allow the worker bees the run of the hive but too fine to allow the much larger queen bee to wander about laying eggs in the honey combs where they could be unwelcome (to you). Above the queen excluder hang the 'supers' in which the honey is stored. These supers are added to as the season progresses and the honey builds up.

It is oddly difficult to remember, as the season progresses, just what is the state of the hives. So keep a card for each hive and make notes of inspection dates, your observations and any alterations to the hive arrangements in the way of extra supers and so on. These cards can be kept in a box with a ball-point pen, the smoker, a box of matches, corrugated paper or cotton rags to fuel the smoker, the hive tool, gloves and other gear.

From April on the hives should be examined every nine days. This is to check for signs of trouble, such as an invasion of wax moth, and to see that the queen is doing her job of egg laying and that grubs are developing in the brood chambers. Queen cells for replacement queens may also be visible; they are much larger than ordinary cells and bulge right out from the edge of the comb. If there is a lack of grubs, this may either mean that the queen is infertile or that the hive is overcrowded, so the beginner should take advice.

The honey is taken at the end of the season, in August/ September. It can either be separated from the wax by using an extractor, or kept and eaten in the comb.

The extractor, which is rather like a spin-drier and whirls the honey out of the comb, is an expensive piece of equipment but it should be possible to hire or even borrow one. The snag is, of course, that everyone wants to extract honey at the same time of the year, so there is considerable competition for extractors.

Once it has been put in jars the honey, which is at first thin and runny, will start to crystallize. If runny honey is preferred, the jars can be put over a very low heat – we stand ours on the back of the Aga, but a saucepan of hot water would do – until the crystallization vanishes. But you cannot quite recapture the perfume of the new honey.

Meanwhile, because you have taken the colony's stores, the bees must be fed. Each hive needs between thirty and sixty lb. of stores to see them through the winter of honey, supplemented if necessary, by syrup made with sugar and water. The syrup goes in a large tin, with a capacity of three or four pints. Punch a lot of small holes around the top, turn it upside down on to a plate and leave it to drip until the syrup no longer runs out. The bees can then help themselves from the little holes. Candy is also provided as emergency food. The food supply should be put in the top of the hive, where the supers were. When the honey has been taken the queen excluder should be removed to allow the queen to move all over the hive; if this is not done the bees stay with the queen in the colder, lower part of the hive and they may die through lack of food and warmth. The queen excluder will not be needed again until the bees start to collect honey in the spring. The bees should be left strictly alone during the winter, with a more than adequate supply. It is permissible to replenish

the store of candy, which can be done without disturbing the
bees if great care is taken.

Avoiding stings

Certain things annoy bees: they are crosser in thundery weather
and when the sky is overcast; they dislike being near pylons; they
hate bangs and vibrations, which is one more reason why hives
should work smoothly. It helps to avoid irritating the bees if the
beekeeper can keep calm and cool while handling them; they seem
more apt to sting hot people. The smoker is a great help when
handling bees: they react to the smoke by stuffing themselves
with honey, which makes them sluggish and good tempered.
Swarming bees always have a good feed before they leave the
hive; they sometimes eat so much that they are unable to curve
their bodies enough to use their stings.

Swarms

It is said that a flying swarm can often be induced to settle by
banging gongs or saucepans, if you are unselfconscious enough
to try this. This is odd because bees are stone-deaf according to
the eighteenth-century naturalist Gilbert White, who tried to
contact them by shouting at the hives through a loudhailer at
very close quarters, without result. Maybe the bees feel the vibrations. Once the swarm has settled, probably on a tree, it can be
shaken or scooped into a box, which is then left upside down near
an empty hive, tilted a little to allow the bees out and on to a
board leading up to the hive entrance; the bees will then find
their own way to their new home.

When examining the bees it is helpful to be able to find the
queen and most amateurs will admit that they find this extremely
difficult. When the bee dealer brings the bees and the queen, you
can ask him to mark the queen with a blob of colouring (or nail
varnish can be used); this would help by showing the look of the
queen and the places where she is likely to be found, while experience is being acquired.

There is another way of keeping bees which, while it cannot be
exactly recommended, does seem to work reasonably well. This
is to have two or three hives, to neglect the bees entirely, looking
at them perhaps three or four times a year, to take what honey
there is, which will be about half what it should be, provide sugar
feed and otherwise to leave the bees very largely to their own
devices.

Bees are endlessly fascinating and beekeeping can become as
complicated as one likes to make it. There are many excellent

books on the subject. Maeterlinck's classic *The Life of the Bee* was until recently available in paperback from Allen and Unwin; it is beautifully written and still gives valuable insight into the strange world of the hive. I hope it will soon be republished. A good, helpful book is *Principles of Practical Beekeeping* by Robert Couston, published by Scottish and Universal Newspapers Ltd., Grange Place, Kilmarnock. The British Beekeepers' Association is also very helpful; it will arrange insurance for a nominal sum and has a useful magazine called *Bee Craft* in which there are always seasonal notes for beginners. See also page 172 for other useful contacts and publications.

Recipes

HONEY

Once the larder is full of honey, it is easy to find plenty of uses for it, apart from spreading it on bread. It makes a good glaze for pork (see page 97) or ham; it is good whisked into an oil and vinegar salad dressing, or melted in a pan with the juice of a lemon and a little water to make a syrup base for a fruit salad, or used as a substitute for treacle in a treacle tart, or stirred into a toddy made with boiling water, whisky and lemon juice – a most comforting drink for someone with a bad cold.

Honey scones

8 oz. (225 g.) plain flour
Salt to taste
3 teaspoons baking powder

2 oz. (50 g.) butter
1 teacup milk (sour, if possible)
½ teacup honey

Sift the flour with the salt and the baking powder. Rub in the butter. Warm the milk and melt the honey in it, then mix with the dry ingredients to make a soft dough. Roll out lightly, not too thin, cut into rounds and bake in a quick oven (450 °F/230 °C/gas mark 8) for about ten minutes, until starting to brown. Take the mout, wrap them in a clean teacloth and eat when they are cool enough.

Honey biscuits

1 cup butter
1 cup sugar
1 egg
1 cup honey

1½ cups plain flour
2 teaspoons baking powder
½ cup chopped crystallized ginger

Cream the butter with the sugar. Beat the egg and add it to the butter and sugar with the honey. Sift in the flour and baking powder and mix in with the crystallized ginger.

Bake in a moderate oven (350 °F/180 °C/gas mark 4) for a quarter of an hour on a greased baking sheet. Put on wire racks to dry thoroughly in a warm place; the biscuits will then keep well in a tin.

CHAPTER SEVEN

Fish Farming

THIS IS a subject which has intrigued me for a long time but the practical difficulties for one who lives on a streamless hill seem to be immense. The Weald around us is full of ponds, man-made for the most part, a by-product of the iron industry which flourished here in the sixteenth century, or created for watering stock. Later the ponds came in useful again as a water source for the huge traction engines which powered agriculture before steam was replaced by oil. Now the ponds are in decay, useless and un-wanted except by naturalists and small boys. For the most part they are too stagnant and polluted to provide a home for fish.

We all know that centuries ago, monasteries and large houses kept ponds stocked with varieties of fish which did not require running water to grow into food for the hungry, dreary winter and the fast days of the Church, but all those lay brothers and peasants must have been kept busy, excavating, dredging and draining to maintain the system. Nor were medieval fish farms handicapped by the fertilizers and other agricultural chemicals which now pollute our ponds. I feel that for us and other part-timers it would not be feasible to construct a twentieth-century system of stew ponds, but were we lucky enough to have a healthy pond, we would certainly stock it with suitable edible fish.

If you are fortunate enough to have a stream running through your land, like Cyril Ayley, a neighbour of ours who has supplied the information below, the story could be very different for you could then consider growing rainbow trout, not so much for fast days as for feast days. In Burgundy I saw a trout farm operating most efficiently. The stream was narrow and the pools were not large, but leaping with fish and looked after by one old man who seemed to bear his responsibilities very lightly. Later we feasted on the deliciously fresh trout.

Without using intensive fish-farming methods it should be possible to use a stream to build up a big stock of fish over two or three years; enough to provide sufficient fish for a family and still leave a surplus to give away to friends.

The rainbow trout is a hardy fish and it grows very fast if you feed it well. It can live in various water temperatures, but it does need moving water of reasonably good quality. If you are uncertain about the water in your stream the fisheries department of your local area water authority could probably test it for you. Assuming that the water is suitable you should form three interconnecting pools in the stream. Starting at the upstream end, the first pool should be about 20 feet long and 5 to 6 feet wide, varying in depth by an easy gradient between a few inches and 2 to 3 feet. This pool is for the fry and should be covered completely with wire netting to thwart fish-eating birds. The middle pool should be around 30 feet long and 10 feet wide, varying in depth between a few inches and 4 feet. This pool is for the yearlings. The downstream pool is the largest and should be around 50 feet long and 15 feet wide to accommodate the two-year-olds and upwards. The depth of this pool should vary between 6 inches and 5 feet. You may need to excavate and widen the stream in places to get the size and shape of each pool right. Ideally, the water should fall a foot or two between each pool as this helps aeration, particularly with a slow-flowing stream.

It will be necessary to construct screens at both the top and bottom ends of the stream to prevent the fish migrating. Screens will also be needed to separate each pool from the other. Screens 3 or 4 feet wide would be about right. For the fry the two screens should be made of perforated zinc, but the others can be constructed of half-inch chicken wire, or for longer life, expanded stainless steel mesh. The screens are placed across the stream at right angles to the bank, but the top edge must fall away downstream so that the plane of the screen is at 45 degrees to the bed of the stream. This has the effect of collecting floating débris, such as leaves, twigs, weeds, etc., at the top of the screen, thus facilitating the easier flow of water underneath. Screens, of course should be cleaned regularly.

With regard to the bed of the stream, it is better to have a natural earth bottom so that it can be planted (but not over-planted) with water-cress, milfoil, crowfoot, etc. Aquatic plants provide shelter for the fish from too bright sun, offer sanctuary to young fish and collect fishfood in the shape of tiny water creatures which live on even tinier water plants called algae.

Of course, a given stretch of water will only support naturally a fraction of the number of fish which can be 'grown' in that same stretch with proper feeding. So it will be necessary to provide food. Any fresh meat will do, but ox liver is the best. For young fry, food must be very finely minced and given to them four or five times a day. As they grow, the meals are gradually decreased and less finely minced, so that when they are three inches long one meal a day will be adequate. At this stage a bigger variety of food becomes available – low-quality white fish or horseflesh mixed with biscuit meal. Various proprietary brands can also be used. The best guide as to the correct amount of food to give the fish is to stop feeding them when they will not take any more at any one time. Any uneaten food will sink to the bottom of the stream and foul the water, so overfeeding is not only wasteful but harmful.

The initial stock of fry for the first year, which should be introduced as available between December and April, should be about five thousand. If you do not have enough land and/or water available to allow for the pools recommended, you could scale them down and the number of fish to be introduced in proportion. All the fry, of course, will not reach maturity and you should allow for a loss of fifty per cent. At the end of the year, the remaining fish, which are now yearlings, should be netted and transferred to the next downstream pool, and a further stock of fry can be introduced into the first pool. You will find that during the second twelve months, if you have fed your fish well, you will be able to use some of the larger ones for table. They are easily caught with a net, being semi-domesticated. At the end of the second year further transfers of stock are made from one pool to the other, and the third pool will now contain your main stock for food purposes to be netted when required.

Supplies of rainbow trout for stocking purposes can possibly be obtained from the fisheries department of your area water authority. If they cannot help, then inquiries should be made of the National Farmers' Union who will only be too pleased to furnish you with the names and addresses of fish breeders and suppliers. It should be borne in mind that any movement of fish from one place to another must be authorized by your area water authority. This is a legal requirement and it is designed to prevent the spread of disease. It is absolutely essential to keep one's stock healthy and the following hints should help in this respect:

1   Do not overcrowd your fish.
2   Do not handle them or frighten them in any way.
3   Do not overfeed them.
4   Keep your ponds and screens clean.
5   Keep water vegetation well in control.
6   If in spite of everything your fish show signs of ailing in any way, seek the advice of the area water authority.

Nothing has been said about breeding rainbow trout, but if you are successful in rearing them, there is no reason why if you are interested, you should not be able to breed them on a small scale as well. There are several excellent books dealing not only with breeding, but fish culture in general, which can be obtained fairly easily:

Textbook of Fish Culture, M. Huet, Fishing News (Books) Ltd., West Byfleet, Surrey.
Trout Farming, D. B. Greenberg, Chilton Co., Philadelphia, U.S.A.
Trout Farming Handbook, S. Drummond Sedgwick, Seeley Service & Co., London.
Aquaculture, J. E. Bardech and others, Wiley Interscience.

Recipes

FISH COOKING

The fish from your own fish farm will be so fresh that the simplest cooking will probably be the best. The fish can be rubbed with olive oil and salt, scored two or three times on each side and then grilled, either in the kitchen or, perhaps best of all, on a charcoal grill in the open air. Or they can be fried in butter and served with a squeeze of lemon and a sprinkling of chopped parsley.

I like to bake trout in the oven, each wrapped in a little envelope of foil. Grease the foil with olive oil, lay the fish on the foil and season each fish with salt, pepper and lemon juice, and sprinkle with chopped fresh dill.

Wrap the fish, put them in a roasting tin and bake in a fairly hot oven (425 °F/220 °C/gas mark 7) for fifteen minutes or so depending on the size of the fish.

They can be served in their envelopes, with good bread to mop up the juices and a green salad to follow.

Two young beekeepers putting a newly caught wild swarm into a hive. Note the irregular shape of the naturally made honeycombs.

Putting the netted fish into a tank for sorting.

Mr Bob Mattin surveying his vegetable garden.

Bringing home the rhubarb.

Glass demi-johns with their bottoms removed can be used in place of expensive cloches.

CHAPTER EIGHT

The Vegetable Garden

THE ROAD to my kitchen garden is paved with good intentions and the reality falls sadly short of my dreams during the winter months when we are ordering seeds, digging and planning. The truth is that growing vegetables successfully takes much time and not a little skill. At the same time it is possible, even in a rather inefficient and lazy way, to grow food and I have learned through many mistakes to stick to four golden rules:

1   Start small.
2   Make a three-year cropping plan.
3   Work *with* the soil and your own limitations and grow crops suitable to it and to you.
4   Do jobs at the right time.

It is a great temptation to clear more ground than you can possibly cope with. Far better to garden intensively in a small area and keep it clean of all weeds, protected from pests and lavishly pampered with compost and dung. However small the plot may be, divide it into sections so that crops can be rotated and prepared for according to their needs. There is nothing to be gained by skirting lush rows of perpetual spinach while you are trying to prepare ground for potatoes. Then be ruthless about the choice of crops. Peas, for example, are difficult to grow and a beginner would be advised to steer clear of them, to concentrate on the prolific broad beans, runner beans and those exquisite French beans.

The seed catalogues are so enticing, and carry the gardener away into a fantasy world where scores of melons dangle in the greenhouse and asparagus spears leap up like dragons' teeth, where there are neither rabbits nor wire worm, nor wood pigeons nor slugs, and where ready-washed vegetables pose for the cameras on the country-style pine dresser.

If the gardener can survive the temptations of the seed catalogues, can start modestly and plan far ahead, then there will be at least some delicious fresh vegetables at all times of the year and if one crop fails, others will succeed.

The vegetable garden, divided into three, could be started with easy crops. The **roots section** could have potatoes, beetroot, carrots and parsnips. It is very likely that there will not be room to grow the main crop of these vegetables, or possibly not the time or inclination to make the necessary clamps or room for the sand-filled boxes in which they can be stored throughout the winter, but at least there will be lovely new potatoes, carrots and beets through the summer and early autumn, and parsnips will carry on through the winter if protected from rabbits and slugs. It is best to lift the remaining parsnips in January or February; perhaps space could be found for these in a peat- or sand-filled box.

The **brassica section** would grow all members of the cabbage family, including swedes and turnips which, although one thinks of them as roots, are in fact brassicas and subject to the same diseases. Easy brassicas are cabbages, Brussels sprouts, sprouting broccoli, kohl rabi and swedes, and possibly turnips too, though these are less hardy than swedes and kale, the easiest of them all. These crops would provide food all the year round.

Into the remaining plot, the **legumes section**, goes almost everything else – onions (more easily grown from sets, that from seed), beans of various kinds, spinach, leeks, shallots, sweetcorn and probably the salad crops of lettuces, radishes and spring onions. This plot is the summer and autumn standby.

Also easy to grow are all the marrows, squashes, courgettes and pumpkins, outdoor tomatoes and outdoor cucumbers, rhubarb, horseradish, Jerusalem artichokes and many herbs. None of these is really suitable for the main vegetable plot. The marrow tribe take up far too much room and trail all over everything. Outdoor tomatoes and cucumbers need special feeding and maximum sun and would probably do best on their own against a wall. Rhubarb and horseradish are perennial plants, as are many herbs, and should not be grown where they will get in the way of other work; horseradish could perhaps go by the compost heap where its vigorous growth will not harm other plants; rhubarb would be easy to incorporate into the border. The marrow tribe is spendidly decorative; the trailing kind can be grown up trellises or over walls where they will adorn any flower garden with their huge flowers, leaves and fruits, while the bush varieties look very handsome in the flower borders, as do many of the herbs. Bay trees, rosemary bushes, sweet laurel and lemon verbena have already found their way into many gardens; the low herbs such as thyme and chives could make pretty and useful edging plants, a welcome change from the eternal lobelias and alyssum, while the taller herbs such as fennel, borage, dill, lemon balm, winter savory and summer savory can be grown among other plants in the flower garden where they are handy for the kitchen.

Should you have a greenhouse it would be easy to grow indoor tomatoes and cucumbers and basil and French tarragon, my favourite herbs, which under glass will flourish for years.

Jerusalem artichokes, if you like their extremely individual taste, are a wonderful winter crop but will smother everything else. It is best to find them a place of their own. The same applies to mint, to which we as a nation are so addicted. Grow the furry mint if you want it to look decorative.

With all these crops there should be a high rate of success in any sunny, well-fed, well-dug soil, so long as the various pests can be warded off.

CROP ROTATION

If, as I recommend, the vegetable garden is divided into three, the rotation goes like this:

Year	Plot 1	Plot 2	Plot 3
FIRST	roots	onions, beans, etc.	brassicas
SECOND	brassicas	roots	onions, beans, etc.
THIRD	onions, beans, etc.	brassicas	roots

The onions, beans and the rest need a very rich, deeply dug well-manured soil.

The roots which follow them, do not do well on soil which has been recently manured but need the richness left behind by last year's manuring.

The brassicas, which follow, should have manure and/or compost. They also need lime, which will sweeten the soil and help to control the dreaded club root, an unpleasant fungal disease to which they are prone.

The lime will persist in the soil the next year, when the plot is planted once more with the beans and other green crops which need it, but by the following year, when the roots are back, the lime will not be present in sufficient quantity to make the potatoes scabby.

SOIL PREPARATION GUIDE

Roots

Dig deep. Lighten and loosen if necessary with ash, gravel, sand.

You can use an all-purpose fertilizer as well, or well-rotted compost, but *not* manure.

Brassicas

Dig early.

Use ground lime. Feed well with dung and/or compost and firm soil thoroughly before planting.

Legumes (Onions, beans, etc.)

Feed liberally with manure and/or compost.

There can be many variations on this basic plan. Very small gardens can be divided into two; an elementary crop rotation would be roots on one half and everything else in the other half. Large gardens could provide all the main crops and so could be divided into four, with potatoes taking up the whole of one plot. But some scheme of rotation is essential to grow good crops, minimize disease and feed and balance the soil.

HARVESTING CHART

Note: I have followed the normal practice of giving **dates which apply to southern counties** – rather unfair, but it has become a gardening book convention, northern gardeners must allow for up to a month's delay in planting dates, and should also allow for earlier frosts in autumn.

When deciding what to grow, the chart on pages 118–19, which shows when various commonly grown vegetables are ready to be eaten, may help. The season for many vegetables can be extended by using a warm greenhouse, or frames or cloches, or a hot bed.

The chart, however, applies to vegetables grown in the open with a little help for tender plants, which can be started off on the kitchen windowsill, a sunny porch, an unheated greenhouse or any other suitable place. The only exceptions are greenhouse tomatoes and greenhouse cucumbers, to be grown in a greenhouse which is usually unheated.

Beetroots, white cabbages, red cabbages, carrots, celeriac, some kinds of marrow, pumpkins, onions, shallots, potatoes, turnips and swedes can all be stored and the roots will keep right through until March, which helps to give some welcome variety. But by March the garden and store are beginning to look somewhat depleted. The chart shows that there is nothing much in the garden in April/May; this is the 'hungry gap', when a dish of young nettles is not to be despised. I always wonder whether nettles are really as good as I think they are, or whether it is simply that they satisfy a craving for something young, fresh and green at that time of the year.

The other point to be noticed from the chart is that many of the vegetables are at their peak just as most of us depart for our holidays. July, August and September are the holiday months as well as the harvest months, and August has the richest, most varied harvest of all. In high summer and early autumn the crops come to perfection so quickly that it is hard to keep pace with them; plenty can be put away in the freezer for the winter and the 'hungry gap'; tomatoes can be bottled, outdoor cucumbers pickled, runner beans salted. So it is quite difficult to fit in a fortnight's holiday.

We always migrate to a Hebridean island in August, where there are very few vegetables. We fill carrier bags with rhubarb, tomatoes, courgettes, beans, cucumbers, beetroots, apples and a few of the more fragile things such as cabbages and lettuces. Herbs are wrapped in damp newspaper and packed into little polythene bags. Friends and family are coerced into looking after garden and greenhouse while we are away. A helpful teenager can often be found to water plants and look after animals for pocket money. Nevertheless, it must be admitted that vegetable gardening and holidays do not mix very well. If you go away early, the vegetables do not get planted; the weeds are leaping up in May and June; if you are away in July, August and September then crops go to waste. But who wants a holiday in November? Some crops can be left out if they do not fit with holiday dates. It is hardly worth bothering with an asparagus bed if you are always away in May, or with sweetcorn if you are off in August.

HARVESTING CHART

January	February	March	April	May	June
Jerusalem artichokes	Jerusalem artichokes			asparagus	
					asparagus
sprouting broccoli	sprouting broccoli	sprouting broccoli	sprouting broccoli		broad beans
Brussels sprouts	Brussels sprouts	spring cabbage	spring cabbage	spring cabbage	spring cabbage
winter cabbage	winter cabbage	winter cabbage			beetroot
winter cauliflower	winter cauliflower	winter cauliflower	winter cauliflower	winter cauliflower	summer cauliflow
trench celery	trench celery				indoor cucumbe
			'hungry gap' kale	'hungry gap' kale	
winter kale	winter kale	winter kale	kale	kale	spring onions
leeks	leeks	leeks	radishes	radishes	shallots
parsnips	parsnips			lettuces	lettuces
winter spinach	winter spinach	winter spinach			mangeto peas
swedes	swedes	turnip tops	turnip tops		peas
					radishes
					summer spinach

	August	September	October	November	December
	broad beans	French beans	runner beans	Jerusalem artichokes	Jerusalem artichokes
…d …s	French beans	runner beans	beetroot	Brussels sprouts	Brussels sprouts
…ch …s	runner beans	beetroot	calabrese		
		calabrese	Brussels sprouts	winter cabbage	winter cabbage
…root	beetroot				
	calabrese		winter cabbage	red cabbage	red cabbage
…mer …age	summer cabbage	summer cabbage		autumn cauliflower	
…ots	carrots	carrots	carrots		
…mer …flower	summer cauliflower	autumn cauliflower	autumn cauliflower	celeriac	
…or …mber	self-blanching celery	self-blanching celery	self-blanching celery	trench celery	trench celery
…ce				winter kale	winter kale
…row	indoor cucumber	indoor cucumber	marrow		
			courgettes	leeks	leeks
…gettes					
…pkins	outdoor cucumber	outdoor cucumber	pumpkins	parsnips	parsnips
		marrow	parsnips	winter spinach	winter spinach
…ns	lettuce				
				swedes	swedes
…ng …ns	marrow	courgettes	main crop potatoes		
	courgettes	pumpkins			
…ots		spring onions	winter spinach		
	pumpkins				
…getout	onions	main crop potatoes	indoor tomatoes		
…toes	spring onions		turnips		
…mer …ach	early potatoes	sweetcorn	swedes		
		indoor tomatoes			
…or …atoes	summer spinach				
…ips	sweetcorn				
	indoor tomatoes	outdoor tomatoes			
		turnips			
	outdoor tomatoes				
		swedes			
	turnips				

PLANTING CHART – using the nurseryman

It is of course also necessary to sow the stuff. If you are short of time, buy in as many of the plants as possible. This saves a great deal of trouble, and you should be able to buy plants which have been reared in warmth, which will give an extended cropping season for many vegetables. The following table shows the dates at which various vegetable seedlings are generally available for planting out – it is all too easy to miss the moment and turn up at the garden shop when all the plants have gone.

Seedling plants commonly available for sale

Globe artichokes	Plant out April
Asparagus	Choose 1-year-old crowns Plant out March/April
Runner beans	Plant out early June
Sprouting broccoli and calabrese	Plant out May/June/July
Brussels sprouts	Plant out first lot late May and second lot June
Spring cabbage	Plant out September/October
Summer cabbage	Plant out May/June
Winter cabbage	Plant out June
Summer cauliflower	Plant out April for an early crop, or June
Autumn cauliflower	Plant out towards end of June
Winter cauliflower (also known as broccoli)	Plant out July
Celery, celeriac	Plant out May/June
Indoor cucumber	Plant in cool greenhouse April/early May or in warm greenhouse March/April
Outdoor cucumber	Plant out early June
Winter kale	Plant out July
Leeks	Plant out June/July
Marrow, courgette	Plant out early June
Sweetcorn	Plant out June
Indoor tomatoes	Plant in unheated greenhouse April/May
Outdoor tomatoes	Plant out May/June

SOWING AND PLANTING CHART

This third chart is for those who are determined to grow vegetables from seed, whenever this is possible. It will be seen that March, April, May and June are the really busy months for sowing and planting – but they are not quite so bad as they look, for probably only some of the vegetables on the chart will be grown and in many cases if you miss the sowing date you will be able to fall back on bought-in plants (see previous chart).

(Dates apply to southern counties)

February

Sow	*Sow*	*Plant*
parsnips	broad beans	Jerusalem artichokes
		shallots

March

Sow	*Sow*	*Plant*
lettuce	Brussels sprouts	Jersualem artichokes
spring onions	mangetout peas	asparagus crowns
radishes	peas	onion sets
onions (seed)	leeks	
parsnips	carrots	
tomatoes (indoor)	spinach	
broad beans		

April

Sow	*Sow*	*Plant*
lettuce	asparagus (seed)	globe artichokes
spring onions	onion sets	asparagus crowns
radishes	parsnips	onion sets
red cabbage	spinach	indoor cucumbers
summer cauliflower	turnips	potatoes
Swiss chard	tomatoes (outdoor)	broad beans for an
peas	broad beans	early crop
sprouting broccoli	autumn cauliflower	red cabbage
Brussels sprouts	mangetout peas	
beetroot (summer use)	summer cabbage	
leeks	carrots	
winter kale	celeriac	

May

Sow	*Sow*	*Plant*
French beans	spring onions	sprouting broccoli
swedes	winter cabbage	
peas		

May (continued)

Sow	Sow	Plant
beetroots (main crop)	autumn cauliflower	Brussels sprouts
winter kale	turnips	summer cabbage
lettuce	radishes	celery
runner beans	sweetcorn	indoor cucumbers
spinach	mangetout peas	
winter cauliflower	asparagus (seed)	
(broccoli)	carrots	
marrows, etc.	Swiss chard	

June

Sow	Sow	Plant
lettuce	peas	outdoor cucumber
swedes	beetroot (main crop)	marrows, etc.
spinach	mangetout peas	sprouting broccoli
spring onions	carrots	summer cabbage
turnips	Swiss chard	celery
runner beans	French beans	Brussels sprouts
		summer cauliflower
		celeriac
		autumn cauliflower
		leeks
		winter cabbage
		red cabbage

July

Sow	Sow	Plant
lettuce	spring onions	winter cauliflower
spinach	'hungry gap' kale	(broccoli)
turnips	spring cabbage	leeks
	parsnips	winter kale
		sprouting broccoli

August

Sow	Sow	Plant
spring onions	winter spinach	—
spring cabbage	turnips for turnip tops	
	onions (seed)	

September

Sow	Sow	Plant
winter spinach	turnips for turnip tops	spring cabbage

October

Sow	Sow	Plant
—	—	spring cabbage

November

Sow	Sow	Plant
broad beans	—	—

BOOKS

There are so many books about the growing of vegetables that I do not propose to go into the details of digging and manuring, the sowing and care of the various vegetables. Very helpful is a well-designed pamphlet called *Vegetable Plotter* by Dr D. G. Hessayan, published by Pan Britannica Industries (who produce various garden sprays and fertilizers) and widely available in many garden shops and seed suppliers. Cheap enough and tough enough to come into the garden with you, its thirty-five pages are packed with information and good advice so simply laid out that it can be absorbed at a glance. Naturally it emphasizes the merits of the judicious use of fertilizers and sprays, particularly those produced by P.B.I.: nevertheless its advice is extremely sound.

For detailed comprehensive instructions on everything to do with the vegetable garden, the Royal Horticultural Society's paperback *The Vegetable Garden Displayed* stands alone. First published in 1941 to help amateurs to Dig for Victory, it has been completely revised and brought up to date and contains about three hundred photographs to illustrate the lucid, well-organized text. There is a list of reminders of work to be done in the garden every month of the year; advice about tools, irrigation, weed control, machinery; cropping plans; a shopping list for seeds and everything you need to know about growing all the vegetables which are commonly grown in this country in an absolutely orthodox way. This book and *Vegetable Plotter* complement each other to fill almost every need.

For original space-saving ideas, try Brian Furner's *Fresh Food From Small Gardens*, published by Stuart and Watkins. There is a recent book (Autumn 1976), edited by John Bond and produced by the staff of Mother Nature, called *The Good Food Growing Guide: Gardening and Living Nature's Way*, published by David and Charles. I have not had time to try out its recommendations, but I am sure it would interest anyone who wants to garden without using artificial fertilizers or pesticides. I am always rather turned off by plans to breed earthworms in the cellar, or even details of the vitamin content of various plants grown in various ways (a legacy perhaps of childhood when one was for ever being told: 'Eat it up, it's so *good* for you.') However, there are many ideas in this book which are fascinating even for the most hidebound and sceptical, for example, suggestions for biological pest control by means of natural predators; recipes for non-poisonous anti-pest sprays; lists of plants which benefit certain other plants and should be grown with them, and lists of plants which have an

adverse effect on certain other plants and should therefore be
kept away from them, and much more.

Brian Furner has written another book about vegetable gardening called *Less Usual Vegetables* (Macdonalds). It is certainly fun
to try to grow these crops, particularly as they are seldom available in the shops, or are very expensive to buy. Here we have
grown golden tomatoes, purple stick beans, lady's fingers, melons,
butter-yellow globe-shaped marrows (delicious, these), mange-
tout peas. However, we do not attempt to grow much which is
difficult or out of the way. Neighbours have been more enterprising, growing such things as potatoes which are purple inside
and out (unreliably claimed to have been developed as suitably
royal fare, during Lent, for some Balkan crowned head), a pro-
fusion of globe artichokes, Hambury grapes, capsicums, chillies
and sea kale.

Finally as an insurance against failure consider *Food for Free*
by Richard Mabey, published by Collins.

Recipes

The kitchen garden provides herbs and vegetables to set off the
food from the poultry and the animals. All the subtlety, charm
and variety of home cooking depends upon it. The variety of
flavours is infinite and I can do no more than mention some of
the many hundreds of ways of using garden produce.

SALAD RECIPES

Winter salads seem especially important in those grey and dreary
days. I have a low opinion of greenhouse lettuces, but there are
many lovely winter salads which, with their robust flavours and
colours, seem to go well with the season.

Beetroot salad
Skin and slice boiled or baked beetroots. Put them in a china
dish with chopped celery and anoint with a garlicky oil and
vinegar dressing (one part vinegar to three of oil). Dust with
chopped parsley.

Mixed root salad
Grate raw carrots, raw turnips and half a raw swede. Crush in

a clove of garlic. Make a salad dressing with fresh lemon juice and olive oil, salt, pepper and mustard. Pound some cumin seed and sprinkle this over the salad. Leave for half an hour before serving.

Watercress and orange salad

The watercress must be absolutely fresh. Put it in a dish. Skin and slice a large orange, removing pips and pith, cut the slices in half and add them to the watercress. Grate in a raw shallot. Squeeze half a lemon and half an orange and add to walnut oil (a most useful thing to have in the kitchen) to make a dressing. Season with salt and pepper and a little brown sugar.

Red cabbage salad

Slice an onion and fry it very gently in bacon fat with a crushed clove of garlic. Slice a red cabbage very finely and put it in a salad bowl with the onion. Grate in a large rather sour apple and add an oil and vinegar dressing. Leave for half an hour before serving.

Cauliflower salad

Divide a cauliflower into florets. Bring a pan of salted water to the boil, drop in the florets and boil for about three minutes, or until barely softened. Drain, put in a bowl and add at once a dressing made from half a tin of anchovies, pounded or mashed well with a clove of garlic, olive oil, white vinegar, pepper, two hard-boiled eggs, chopped, and a little salt, remembering the saltiness of the anchovies. Leave to cool.

Butter bean salad

This can be made with any dried beans which may have been stored at the end of the summer.

Soak the beans until they have swollen. Drain, add fresh water, parsley, thyme and bay leaf and an onion, whole, and cook very gently, adding no salt to the pan (salt toughens the skins). When nearly ready, add salt and allow to cook for a further half hour.

Drain, put in a bowl and at once add plenty of garlic and a highly seasoned olive oil and wine vinegar dressing into which you have stirred a generous spoonful of either a spiced mustard (such as Moutarde de Meaux) or creamed horseradish.

This is another salad which improves with keeping; it will be even better the day after it was made.

SOUP RECIPE

A mushroom soup for a mushroom glut

Mushrooms do not strictly speaking come from the garden, but when they cover the fields around, they will make into this soup, which is too good to leave out.

3 lb. (1·3 kg.) of field mushrooms   A squeeze of lemon
A scrape of butter   1 dessertspoon creamed
Salt and pepper   horseradish
½ pint (3 dl.) of chicken stock   2 tablespoons cream
½ pint (3 dl.) of milk

Wash the mushrooms and put them in a heavy, buttered pan. Add seasoning. Leave them to cook slowly in their own juices until very soft. Add the stock and put the soup in the liquidizer or sieve it, or put it through the vegetable mill. Return to the pan, add the milk to make the soup of the required thickness, add the lemon juice and horseradish, and taste to check the seasoning. Float the cream on the top just before serving.

CHAPTER NINE

Using the Grass from the Garden

THE MOST valuable crop from the garden is, undoubtedly, grass. It will grow anywhere and yield several crops every year. It can be turned into meat by animals and geese; into eggs by poultry; even into fun and exercise by a pony. It can easily be dried for winter use in the form of hay, or fermented and stored as silage. So it is worth some thought and careful planning to ensure that full use can be made of the grass while not spoiling the look of the garden.

If, like a farmer, you wish to produce the maximum amount of grass with the minimum amount of effort, the course is quite clear: fell the trees and clear the scrub to allow light; drain well; plough up and sow a suitable grass mixture; fertilize heavily – and watch it grow. But then you would not have a garden.

Some compromise there will have to be. If it is possible, clear some of the scrubbier trees, leaving a few beautiful specimens, and restrict delicate flowering shrubs to one or two small areas which could be fenced or walled off. Poisonous plants such as yew and laurel must be banned. Another poisonous plant to look out for is ragwort, a common weed, luckily very noticeable as it is tall, one to two feet high, with bright yellow flowers. Grazing animals will not touch growing ragwort but if it is in the hay it is sometimes eaten, with fatal results.

Spring bulbs are fine unless hay is to be made, for grazing animals will not eat the leaves, but again if the hay is full of daffodil leaves it will not be very good for the animals. If the bulbs are kept to small areas, planted round the trunks of trees, they can be left uncut.

Trees, once established, will not suffer from most grazing animals, with the exception of goats which tend to eat the bark. Horses and ponies can also chew bark although most do not. If bark chewing does occur, buy a Treebark Protector, a foul-smelling stuff to paint on to the chew marks and put the animals off. It can be ordered from the Country Gentlemen's Association (see page 170). Animals will, however, nibble at the lower branches of trees. This does no harm, but does of course alter the shape of the tree.

Young trees are a different matter and when planting trees in an area which is to be grazed it is essential to protect them either by those rather nice old-fashioned iron tree guards (also available at a price from the Country Gentlemen's Association) or by a ring of stout fencing.

Areas which are not suitable for grazing either because of the presence of shrubs, or because they are too small or too awkward to fence, or because you are going to want to sit in them and you do not fancy sitting among animal droppings, may well be excellent for hay. But don't take hay from near yew trees or yew hedges.

How to look after grass

1   Once a sward is established, weeds will not thrive so long as the grass is not killed by bonfires, fallen trees, piles of rotting cut grass, leaves and the like, and so long as the grass is kept short by regular grazing and/or cutting.
2   The quality of the grass is always improved by frequent cutting or grazing. A common farming practice is to cut or graze every three to five weeks during the growing season.
3   To increase the grass yield, fertilizers can be used; more of this later.
4   Gardens often suffer from lime deficiency. Soil analysis will easily determine whether this applies to your garden. Lime deficiency must be put right, or growth will be poor and fertilizers considerably less effective.

Grazing

The grazing should be divided by fencing to allow each area to rest between grazings. Should your garden be large enough to

Collecting the wild harvest: above, picking elderflowers for wine; below, sorting field mushrooms for the freezer.

Building hay around a tripod.

A suitable prop for the ventilating holes.

A garden gate stall. How many proprietors of such stalls know the regulations?

keep a cow, she should have first bite, followed by the sheep, and then by the geese. Move the creatures on when they have cleared up the grass, apply fertilizer (if it is to be used) immediately the animals have been moved, and rest the grass, which grows up again. Ideally the animals should return after three to five weeks.

In very difficult conditions, such as the notorious drought of 1976, the whole arrangement goes awry, for the grass simply does not grow. But in the normal British summer, provided that you do not have more animals than the land can cope with, the grass will continue to grow throughout the summer and it will grow particularly fast during the spring and autumn. So farmers make hay and silage in the early part of the season and probably take a further cut of silage in the autumn, and still hope to have enough grazing.

Animals graze in different ways. The cow wraps her tongue around rather long thick grass and shovels it in in large bunches. She then passes on, making cow pats at frequent intervals. She will not graze near the cow pats, so weeds and tall tufts of grass grow up around them. Sheep will eventually demolish these tufts and graze close to the ground, leaving a beautiful close cropped sward. Geese will eat even more closely than sheep and also nibble away at certain weeds, so they will improve the quality of a lawn – if you can put up with their messy droppings, which of course improve the lawn further.

None of these creatures will eat coarse weeds such as thistles, docks or nettles, so it is sound practice to cut these with the mower once or twice during the season, before they seed. This is known as 'topping'. Selective weedkillers can be used, as they are on lawns.

Fertilizing

Growing grass needs nitrogen, potash and phosphates. The dung of grazing animals is rich in potash and phosphates, not surprisingly as these are the nutrients which were removed with the crop by the animals themselves. The nitrogen is to stimulate growth. It can either be provided in artificial form, or by plants, particularly clovers, which are capable of absorbing it from the air.

Most farmers would agree that they cannot produce the crops of grass which are necessary to support, say, a herd of heavy milking cows, without the use of artificial nitrogen; clovers alone simply will not produce enough nitrogen, and attempts to supplement artificially merely kill the clovers.

The garden-farmer may well feel that heavy crops of grass are

I

Fencing. 1. A strong way of stapling wire to the post. **2.** The corner posts and those beside gateways should be strengthened against the pull of the wire by supporting stakes as shown. The foot of the supporting stakes can be further strengthened by a 12-inch long stake hammered right into the ground. **3.** The drivall, a useful tool for

4

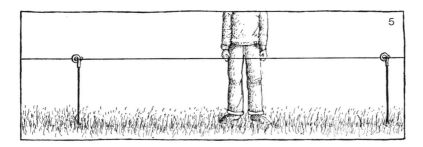

5

6

driving in posts, to be used instead of a sledge hammer. **4.** Chestnut paling. **5.** Electric fencing with insulated supports, which can be run either off a battery or the mains. Not to be used with sheep. **6.** Using a wire strainer to tighten barbed wire.

not necessary for a backyard operation. Artificial fertilizers are expensive and the whole thing becomes more of a business than a hobby. But in case anyone suddenly wants to keep four large ewes on one acre of ground, or make a lot of hay, here is how it is done:

1 What does the land need?

Find out what the land needs by soil analysis, either by using a soil sampling kit bought from a local garden centre, or by sending away samples for analysis. A local farmer would be able to supply an address for this, or you can simply ask advice from a neighbouring farmer who will probably have a shrewd idea of what the land needs without the help of a soil sample.

2 How much?

Go to a supplier to buy the necessary fertilizer. Don't buy more than is necessary, for it can get damp and then brick-hard, when it is useless.

Fertilizers are sold in polythene sacks and there is a certain amount of 'units' to each sack; this number varies according to the make and balance of the fertilizer and information is given on the sack. If in doubt, ask the supplier how many 'units' per sack there are in the fertilizer you want.

Then work out how much to buy. The farming rule of thumb is:

Apply two units of nitrogen per acre per day that the grass will be resting.

So if a farmer has taken his cows off one acre of grass, planning to bring them back after three weeks, he will apply forty-two units of nitrogen – two units for every day of the three weeks that the cows will be away.

Hay and silage take far more out of the soil than grazing animals do, so give a generous dollop of nitrogen in March when your hay paddock should be shut away from the animals to allow the grass to grow. Be prepared, also, to put on a compound fertilizer (one that contains not only nitrogen but potash and phosphate). The amount will depend on whether you use the paddock for grazing later in the season or not, so take advice.

Later, after a second period of using the grass, the whole operation can be repeated, always remembering there is less response to nitrogen in the dry, late summer.

3 When to use fertilizers

Grass takes up the fertilizer as it grows; it is wasted if applied when the grass is not growing. So fertilizers should be used in the spring and early summer and not in the late summer when the grass is growing slowly, as stated above. This is a general rule only – in our climate it is impossible to be too dogmatic.

4 How to apply fertilizer

A large area, such as the paddock described in the chapter on how to keep a cow, might have to be done by contract, but a small area could be tackled by the family scattering the stuff out of buckets as evenly as possible.

5 Caution

Nitrogen can be poisonous to grazing animals when used heavily, so it would be wise not to let animals in until two weeks after applying nitrogen.

HAY FROM THE GARDEN

The best hay is made from young grass. So forget about the thigh-deep hayfield, full of flowers and pollen. Well-made hay, when the grass is young and leafy and the drying has been even and complete, has enormously greater feeding value than hay which has been cut late and allowed to burn in the sun on one side and rot on the ground on the other. It is not the weight or quantity of hay that will get your ewe through the winter to bear twin lambs in the spring and rear them, but the quality.

It is extremely difficult to buy good hay. Farmers keep it for their own stock. For selling purposes they often wait until the grass has grown long and bulky; the hay looks the same in the bale and that way they have more bales to sell. So, if there is reasonably good grass in the garden, the garden-farmer is far better off making his own hay, and as he is making hay by hand in small quantities he can achieve a perfection which eludes the busy farmer, with all his gaily painted and expensive tackle.

Cutting

Wait for a spell of fine weather in early or mid-June, when the grass is in head but not flowering, let alone seeding.

Small areas can be cut with a scythe. Scything is an art in itself and one that is well worth acquiring. A big scythe, kept razor-sharp and in the hands of someone who knows how to use it is a very efficient mower that uses no petrol, never breaks down and covers the ground at a surprising pace. With a bit of practice more or less anyone can use a scythe effectively if roughly, so long as the blade is properly aligned with the handle so that a swing of the arms carries the blade evenly just above the ground, in a long semi-circular sweep. Scything is easier when the dew is still on the grass.

On banks or awkward places, a sickle or swap hook can be used to cut the grass. Larger areas can be tackled with a bar cutter machine such as an Allen scythe, or the cutting can be done by contract as a last resort. It is a last resort because in ideal haymaking weather you will have to wait your turn and this could be disastrous if the weather does not hold. After machine cutting, tidy up the corners and under shrubs by hand.

Making the hay

When the grass is cut, leave it lying, turning it with a prong (pitchfork) as may be necessary, shaking it up in the air, leaving it fluffed up so that the breeze can blow through it. The test of when to turn the grass is to see whether it looks different on the top from the underside. The aim is to dry the grass absolutely evenly. Any obstinate bit of clover or very lush grass that lags behind the rest must be carefully laid on top, or taken out of the swathe.

It requires some self-control to leave the hay until it is completely ready and much good hay has been ruined by being carted just too soon. The exciting moment comes when the hay begins to rustle as it is turned, but don't assume too rashly that it is ready. A humid, cloudy night can transform hay that a few hours earlier, in brilliant sunshine, seemed perfect to a drab limpness. It is wise to go on a few hours longer after that first encouraging rustle.

The timing of course depends entirely on the weather and the thickness of the crop. The best conditions for haymaking are sun and wind together. In brilliant sunshine and very low humidity it can be made in a day, turning it probably every hour. In duller weather it can be made in three or four days, but then it would not need turning half so often. The quicker the hay is made, the better it will be.

The hay should finally be stored under cover, in a shed or loft, but before storing it should be allowed to weather outside for a few weeks, for if stored prematurely it can heat up and the quality of the hay will be ruined; it can even start a fire by spontaneous combustion. So it will have to be left in the fresh air in a way that will protect it from the weather.

The simplest way to do this is to pile it into haycocks. Rake up some hay and spread some in a circle on the ground, about five feet across. Now the aim is to build up the haycock to about six or seven feet in height, in a conical pointed shape rather like an old-fashioned straw beehive. The hay is put on loosely to allow the fresh air in, but the haycock must be steady and well balanced. So, using a prong, lay on forkfuls of hay, working spirally round and round the base and always keeping the outside of the heap rather higher than the inside. Then shape it off to a point at the top, comb down the hay on the outside of the cock with the prong so that the rain will run down the cock and not into it, and then, if the hay is in a windy exposed place, finish it off by tying it down with string weighted with bricks or stones. Some people cap their haycocks with a piece of polythene and this too should be held down with weighted string. Well-made hay can be left in haycocks for weeks without coming to any harm.

A more sophisticated method is to tripod the hay. A tripod is a haycock built around a frame. Three bean poles can be tied together near the top and stood up to make a tripod. Twine string around the tripod legs and you have a cage which will allow fresh air to circulate right through the hay. Then build up the haycock all round the frame, burying it completely. A through draught is encouraged by propping open two air holes at the bottom of the tripoded hay on opposite sides; use old bits of drain pipe, or clay ridge tiles, or anything else which may be lying around. The point of the tripoding method is to allow the wind to get in under the haycock and into its centre, and so keep it dry in all weathers.

When the time comes to store the hay for the winter it will have to be transported somehow. On a garden scale this could be done by inviting a lot of people to lunch with their wheelbarrows, or it could be done by two people with a big garden trolley. These trolleys are fiendishly expensive to buy, but prove a boon for all sorts of jobs to anybody with a large garden. Alternatively, it might be worth getting the hay baled and carried by contract. It depends on the size of the job.

GARDEN SILAGE

Silage is grass (or other edible vegetable matter, but usually it is made with grass) which has been pressed down to exclude the air, protected from the air and allowed to ferment. It will then keep indefinitely and is excellent food for stock. There are now many additives on the market which break down the bacteria and assist the silage-making process, which need only be used when the grass is wet, or very young and leafy. Silage requires a container to exclude the air, either a bunker of some sort, which could have wooden walls, or be tunnelled out of a bank so that the earth forms the walls, or of polythene or some other material. The grass is then put in as quickly as possible, compressed either by rolling or by heavy weights, any additive put on from a watering can in layers, and the heap then covered with polythene, the sheet being weighted down to exclude all air. The silage, when made, should be the colour of tobacco and be dry when squeezed, but animals will eat quite inferior silage with relish. The heap should not be opened up for a few weeks after it is completed. Grass, however, can be added at will so long as the heap is carefully covered over again each time.

Lawn mowings, which are so fine that they are easy to press down, would be the best source of silage for the garden farmer, and they would be suitable for polythene sack silage. They can be pressed into the sacks which are then sealed. This is thought to be a new idea, but a Mr Woods, the enterprising steward of Lord Walsingham, was making silage in barrels at Merton Hall in Norfolk in the 1880s. He wrote:

> Two years ago we put a quantity of chaffed grass and other material into casks, ramming it down compactly, and weighting it and covering it with bran, as in the silos. The result was so satisfactory that last year we extended the experiment, using casks of various sizes. The ensiled material consisted of maize, oats, brank sparrey and common grass. The casks were filled at different times between July and September, an operation easily, economically and expeditiously performed. When opened in the present year the contents were found to be sound and good.

The point of making silage is that success does not depend on the weather, while rain will of course destroy hay that is on the ground. There is no more heartbreaking task than spreading out the wet hay, now brown and evil smelling, turning it miserably from time to time and when it is finally dry, bundling it up into a heap to use as inferior fodder or litter. But it cannot be denied that making silage is rather a business, while hay-making, given reasonable grass and reasonable weather, is pure delight.

CHAPTER TEN

The Uses of Trees

Beechwood fires are bright and clear
If the logs are kept a year.
Oaken logs burn steadily
If the wood is old and dry.
Chestnut's only good, they say
If for long it's laid away.
But ash new or ash old
Is fit for a Queen with a crown of gold.

Birch and fir logs burn too fast,
Blaze up bright but do not last.
Make a fire of elder tree,
Death within your house you'll see.
It is by the Irish said
Hawthorn bakes the sweetest bread.
But ash green or ash brown
Is fit for a Queen with a golden crown.

Elmwood burns like churchyard mould,
E'en the very flames are cold.
Poplar gives a bitter smoke,
Fills your eyes and makes you choke.

Applewood will scent your room
With an incense-like perfume.
But ash wet or ash dry
For a Queen to warm her slippers by.

HAVING A HUSBAND who is fanatical about trees I have left this chapter to him. Where our trees are concerned I provide only the unskilled labour, enthusiastically chopping, sawing and making bonfires, enjoying the exercise and the lovely smell of wood and wood smoke, but in a brainless way, never thinking of where the next log is coming from. But for Alan, reared in almost treeless industrial Yorkshire, trees, those 'reverend vegetables' as Edward Fitzgerald called them, cannot be taken for granted but must be cherished intelligently. The huge cycle of planting, tending and felling the long-lived hardwood trees must be kept turning; now that the big landowners have no longer the resources or the confidence to plant slow-growing trees which will not mature for many human generations, it becomes the responsibility of all of us who have enough room to plant perhaps just one oak, beech, lime or Spanish chestnut which after three hundred years may be spreading giant boughs – over what? To plant one of these trees is to defy the prophets of doom with a ludicrous but touching optimism.

Alan Smith Writes:

If your garden farm includes mature trees and hedgerows then you start with capital in hand and are indeed fortunate. Just standing where they are, they can give shade and shelter, yield fruits for food and drink, produce fuel and compost. The bottom of an old hedgerow is the best of all compost, laid down by nature for a thousand years or more.

You can farm an annual cash crop from your trees – timber, fruits, mistletoe, holly, dried bay leaves for the herb basket, bundles of twigs, bags of logs and sawdust to sell at the garden farm gate. Proper farming of your trees improves the capital value of your property (tax-free), saves money on fuel, and you can enjoy yourself at the same time.

To maintain trees well is a long-term business, needing much thought. We study, sometimes for years, before cutting any and we work hard at caring for those we have and planting for the future. There is a basic rule when felling – if more is taken out than is put in you create a desert. Careful gleaning, pruning, thinning and planting will improve wood resources. Plant at least two trees for every one you fell.

There may be legal restrictions on the felling or planting of trees, but even if there is none, it is neighbourly to bear in mind other people's enjoyment. Remember too that future generations will enjoy today's young growth. After all, most of the trees that we farm today were deliberately planted by our forebears. It is usually a mistake to think of them as self-sown.

We learned about trees the hard way. Cherished plum trees died mysteriously. Why? Probably because their roots, which were close to a wall, dried out in exceptionally dry weather. A lopsided apple tree fell over. A copper beech died when we planted it because we did not water regularly. An ash near the garage grew too big and although we chopped the branches back from the building we did not realize that in a dry summer the roots were sucking all the moisture from the ground. The ground contracted and the building slipped sideways. The virginia creeper, so pretty in autumn, broke up gutters and roof tiles as it grew out of sight, while its falling leaves blocked gutters and caused floods. Shrub roots broke into underground drains, which collected leaves as they swirled through and we were flooded out. An oak which collapsed in a storm cut the power cables and telephone wires and blocked us in the house for hours before we cut our way out. We decided we had to fight back, learn about trees and make them work for us, not against us. So we became tree shepherds.

From our 'flock' every year we now have free jams, tisanes, herbs and wines and honey for the larder; shelter, shade, bedding and food for our animals; compost, staking poles, pea boughs and fencing for the garden. Above all, we save lots of money every winter on our fuel bills.

TREES FOR FUEL

We found out how to do this when oil, electricity, gas and coal were soaring in price. The age of cheap fossil fuel is over unless 'free' sources of power such as tidal mills, solar heaters, wind generators, hot-rocks heating, and their back-up storage systems, come into general use – in which case the price of fossil fuels might drop just in order to remain competitive. But we did not want to go broke paying the oil bill whilst waiting for this to happen nor did we want to shiver in a new ice age as we did in our youth. Perhaps we were not so well fed then, perhaps the winters were more severe, but certainly houses were not heated so well. I remember green mould on my bed in Yorkshire and Joanna remembers putting on overcoats to walk along passages.

First, we improved the nutritional value of the food we ate, then in really hard weather we opened up fireplaces which had been sealed off when central heating was cheap and started to cut enough wood for them. A lot of heat was generated, for wood warms you twice, they say, once in the cutting, once in the burning.

When we improved at keeping the home fires burning we cut and stacked our wood one year and used it the next. Sap in timber leads to poor burning, particularly in open fires, except for ash which is good new or old. So when you switch to wood fuel start the first year with ash and cut and stack the other timber. After a year it has dried out, is lighter to handle and you avoid nasty tar deposits in the chimney, caused by burning green wood. When the fuel crisis was new, many people with solid-fuel burners used green wood with unfortunate results, for after a few months an evil deposit started to ooze out of cracks in the flue pipe and there was a greatly increased fire risk.

To achieve best results in open wood fires it helps to store by type, because woods burn in different ways with different smells, and for fireplaces of different sizes the wood should be cut to lengths in advance.

John Wyatt, author of *The Shining Levels* (published by the Gamstone Press), is a connoisseur of wood smoke:

For fragrance, in my opinion, there is little to match juniper; I would stack this wood aside against the days I had visitors. Apple and well-seasoned cherry are pure luxury too. Holly and birch have a clean tang. Ash, particularly green ash, smells like washing day. Old oak has an honest, pungent, lusty smell as you would expect. The other hardwoods are hardly worth a mention smokewise. The soft woods; pine, spruce or larch are rather vulgar; but there is something to be said for a really old vintage larch root.

Once one gets the taste for smoking wood it is possible to mix and obtain subtle flavours, and invent recipes: prepare a fire base of larch kindling; add well-seasoned oak until the logs redden deeply; place one large back-log of holly, and add, from the fire back to the front, one crab-apple log, one of well-dried cherry and one of birch. An ideal after-dinner mixture.

Despite the success of our open-fire policy, so much heat was lost up the chimney that we still used background central heating and during the fuel crisis we reached the stage when we winced every time we heard our boiler fire. When we felt we could not stand it any longer I suddenly said: 'I don't believe the Scandinavians spend money like this – I'm going to the Norwegian embassy.' There they told me about their wood-burning stoves

– slow-burning stoves. We visited an importer in Wales, bought one immediately (for his house was beautifully warm), and installed it in our hall.

Altogether, the Jøtul stove cost us £225, and we have never spent money better. The stove is decorative, requires little attention and gives as much or as little heat as we require. We think we saved that £225 in six months and are warmer than before.

The Jøtul stands one foot out from the wall, two feet six inches high. A pipe inset into a blocked-up chimney takes the smoke away. It is made of metal asbestos and its great virtue is that it hardly ever needs cleaning as setting the stove to 'hot' burns off all deposits in the chimney which then fall back as a fine dust into the stove. The piping is expensive, and the less you need to use the better. The most economical method is to board in an old fireplace and position the stove against it so that only one length is needed. We were not so fortunate and £40 out of the £225 went on piping the stove to pick up a chimney on the first floor.

The stove seems to burn any sort of wood – most sizes and species, though here again it is better not to burn green wood; our dead elm does particularly well. If we need background heat only then it needs filling twice in twenty-four hours; for more heat it needs filling more often. The logs can be as much as two feet long and that saves work on the sawing. They burn on the cigar principle, starting at one end and slowly moving along. They burn so thoroughly that only a shovelful of ash every now and then needs removing – straight on to the garden of course. So the stove can even stand on a carpet as there need be little mess, though it's safer to put a drip tray underneath the entrance to catch any pieces as you load it.

There are other stoves on the market. Some systems now available burn all household wastes and heat the water as well as the house. Some have a plate on top for a kettle on the hob, Others have sliding doors which expose the flames so that it is possible to have the comfort of the open fire as well as the economy of the slow burner.

These stoves get the best out of the wood they are given and this is important to us, for we have no wish to deplete our garden farm's fuel resources. We need to make the most of every twig we have.

After a gale the whole family gleans the orchard. The end of winter is another good time to glean anything from small twigs to big branches; this clears the ground for the grass to grow. Midsummer is the time to look for fallen fir cones and pine needles. The resin in them and their dry nature makes them especially useful for starting fires. A handful of pine needles or a piece of a pine branch thrown on to the fire after dinner will make a pleasant crackling and an attractive smell. As well as gleaning we cut some timber, for some species of trees, ash for example, grow so fast that every year thinnings can be made. If cut about two feet above the ground a tree will spring up again and is ready for felling again in a few years. A few trees we fell outright because they have grown too close together, and if trees are to be beautiful they need space. Other cutting we do because branches hang too low, beginning to shade places where shade is not wanted – the vegetable garden for example.

In areas affected with elm disease, felling and re-planting is of paramount importance. Contrary to popular belief we find elm is excellent fuel. It is best to weather elm for a year before cutting it for the fire as its tight grain makes it hard work. Elm is a marvellous tree with wood of outstanding properties for use in pulleys and blocks. Provided it is kept continuously wet it lasts almost for ever – the wooden walls of the old-time navy were elm and the thousand-year-old piles of London Bridge found still upright in the Thames were elm. The elm disease itself does not affect the timber nor will it affect anything in the house.

Our wood is carted in lengths to the storage area and broken up there in order to minimize handling and reduce the mess in the garden which leads to patches of nettles and docks. We have two stores: one is a bulk store, under cover in the back yard; the other, which is outside the front door, is an old shop-counter converted by being given a lid and divided into sections and standing on bricks. From here the fuel is conveniently dealt out by size and species for the various fires. We used to cut wood anyhow, across a wheelbarrow for example, but to do the job quickly and safely the only answer is a traditional saw horse. Ours has a permanent position, and marks on the ground beneath the cut-off enable the timber to be cut to the exact size of the various grates, so that minimum work is involved. We place the horse over a smooth surface because the sawdust is gathered and used for litter for the animals, as a mulch to keep weeds down, or where there is little compost in the soil, as a thick covering at the start of winter which keeps the heat in and makes earlier crops possible. We rake it off at the end of the winter and it goes straight into the compost heap. The chippings and twigs are stored in paper sacks. They are then carried straight into the house to start fires as needed.

Wood burns best in an ash bed. A big, open-style fire simply needs nursing along on the bottom of the grate until there are enough ashes – or a shovelful from the bonfire would help – and then regular fires are easily maintained for three or four weeks and the ash bed is a foot or more high before any needs removing. A fire dog on both sides helps in the positioning of logs, which are always better placed in parallel so that they fall into the heart of the fire. A fire basket makes a smaller fire possible; it is neater and usually comes further into the room.

It is always easy to buy a load of wood in if we fall behind with the cutting programme. But it is expensive and can only be recommended as a supplement to one's own wooding. It is even more expensive if you are sold short as I once was. The load did not look right but I could not think how to weigh it until we remembered the weights and measures inspector. He came at once and was keen to prosecute when he said I was 6 cwt. out of a ton short. Unfortunately I had left it too late because a prosecution has to be commenced within a certain number of days of delivery.

TREES AND YOUR ANIMALS

Apart from providing fuel, your trees, animals and vegetables have to be induced into mutually beneficial co-existence.

Trees and shrubs in the garden farm provide shade from the sun and shelter from the wind for animals. Of course sun shades can easily be knocked up – a hurdle on four poles, against the angle of a fence or wall for example – but the right trees in the right place are more lasting and aesthetically pleasing. Include trees in the poultry run and chickens will make dust baths around the trunks and between the roots. They literally dig themselves into the soil. This will kill the tree if they go too deep, but bricks dropped into the dust holes or wire buried just under the surface will prevent too much damage.

Ducks and geese will join up with the chickens for their siesta in the shade, so a dish of water fairly nearby is useful. Sitting broodies need to be given shelter from the full heat of the sun so the broody box can be sited under a tree. Alternatively, to knock the broodiness out of a chicken she can be put in an airy box and hung from the branches of a tree. Sheep and pigs find shade essential. Pigs will die if they get too hot, and sheep lose weight.

There are other dangers to trees than chickens in dust baths. Pigs give the impression that they are digging down to Australia and will disappear underground completely except for their tails. Originally they were woodland animals. All the clearings or dens in the forest around me were made by or for the medieval pig – a much smaller hedgehog-like creature than today's extreme versions. The narrow, twisting, deep lanes in this part of the Weald were made by generations of pigs being slowly driven down from the outskirts of London for fattening on autumn mast and acorns before being driven back to London kitchens. For many animals acorns are poisonous but pigs, goats and wood pigeons love them, and they flavour the meat deliciously.

Today's pig in the garden farm can have no such freedom. If kept for more than a few months continuously in the one area it will exhaust the easily-gathered grubs and roots and will go for the main roots and bark. This attack, plus the raw dung, will cause the tree to die, I'm told. I like trees too much to have tested this information, and in consequence never keep pigs in their paddock long enough to exhaust it. To make doubly certain, fence off trees well away from the trunk. Of course if there is scrubland to clear, a pig is an excellent bulldozer, though he may need some help. One way to clear bad bramble patches is to scatter food deeper and deeper into it so that the pig follows the food.

Goats are bad for trees. They eat the bark and succulent shoots. Goat-proofing is almost impossible. With the bark gone the tree will die, and this risk must be kept in mind when deciding to run goats with trees.

Of course animals are not the only ones to harm trees – man himself is a great menace through carelessness and indifference. A tree that is badly treated will be susceptible to disease and an unbalanced tree is likely to blow down. This really causes trouble, because the stump is difficult to get rid of and may prove a source of fungus infection. Trees will collapse even on quite calm days; a horse chestnut, for example, can topple with the weight of rainwater on its dense leaves in summer as a result of imbalance. *Never* use trees as fencing posts – the nails, buried by the growth of the tree, can lead to appalling accidents if at any time a chain saw is used on the timber.

Litter for poultry is provided by leaves, which can be a golden harvest. Ignore them and they block ditches, drains and gutters. We ignored them at first, until we found that everything growing under where they settled for the winter was killed and one rainstorm the water stormed down the drive and flooded the cellar because the drains were choked.

Leaves should be treated as a crop and harvested. If there is not enough there will be no difficulty in finding people who will be delighted to permit gathering until they too realize the value of the gold in dead leaves.

Like corn gleaning, leaf gathering is a case of many hands

making light work, and everyone has fun. One person with an inadequate rake on a windy day feels like Freya and her sieve. Rake the leaves into piles, preferably against leaf traps (the angles of fences or walls), then stuff paper feed-sacks with dry leaves, especially those of beech or oak. Evergreens will not do as the leaves should be absorbent. Store the gathered leaves and use them as litter in the poultry shed or to cover a run which has been scratched bare and which gets too muddy in winter. There will be myriad insects there and so many happy foraging hours for poultry. Man always used leaves for litter until recent times and the price of straw makes the old ways more attractive again.

Leaves can also be stored and used for mulching raspberries and gooseberries at the right time. A leaf mulch is cheaper and prettier than black polythene. Still more leaves can go into a long-term compost heap. They take about two years to break down in the ordinary way. But the result is worth waiting for and is an essential part of the recipe for making your own potting compost.

THE BONFIRE

The bonfire is a very important part of life in the garden, as it has both utility and family appeal. Children love making bonfires and leaving it to them once they have been shown how to build it is a good way of keeping everybody working and happy, though I always stay close while it is burning. Even the hot embers need watching: some went down my son's boots once as he was stamping the fire out in the approved manner and burnt him.

The site of the bonfire needs choosing very carefully. It needs to be sheltered but not windless, as a breeze always helps it to burn briskly whilst a gale either blows it out, burns it out too quickly, or is positively dangerous. Anything overhanging will die back so this should be borne in mind if the site is in a clearing. Some gardeners have a wandering site over the vegetable patch. Each bonfire sterilizes the soil underneath and its ashes can be spread around with the minimum of work. As soon as the bonfire has cooled the ashes should either be covered, stored or spread immediately, or the valuable potash will be leached into the soil with the first rains.

Nobody taught me to build a bonfire. Until last year this was not difficult to see. My bonfire was a heap which all too often burned out in the middle and then had to be started all over again – all very time consuming and irritating until I read John Wyatt's recipe, which helps a little with bonfires and a lot with fires in the house. He says:

K

I have won several bets in my time from workmates, by starting a fire outdoors, in heavy rain, without the use of any dry medium such as paper. The trick is easy if there are birch trees about; then there is always an abundance of dead twigs which can be snapped easily off the trunks. From these can be gathered a handful of needle-thin stuff that can be pushed into a pocket while you collect slightly thicker material. A good pile is made of the birch twigs; then, when all is ready, the handful of needle-thins is taken from the pocket (where they have left much of their moisture), put into the fire centre, and carefully lit with a match. The wood contains sufficient natural oil to start the fire well.

Simpler and for everyman is Bert's advice and method, given to Thomas Firbank (*Log Hut*, Harrap, 1954).

Bert has a feeling for a fire. He rummaged in his pocket for a couple of bills and a rate demand, screwed the papers into loose balls, and set them in a little clear space. He did not pick sticks off the ground, which receive the earth's dampness in all but the longest droughts, but snapped dead twigs off live trees. He selected bits no thicker than matches and laid them patiently in a tepee construction about his paper. One match started a clear flame, and an infant crackling began. He added more dead wood from the standing trees; this time pieces as thick as a finger.

Now Bert added dead wood off the ground, careless of its dampness. But he was particular to snap it across his knee into even lengths of a couple of feet or so, and to lay it all in the same direction, following the course of the breeze.

FRUITS AND HERBS

No garden farm should be without certain specific trees and shrubs. The most useful of all is the elderberry, and there should be no difficulty in establishing this. It is almost a tree weed. Traditionally it was to be found near the larder as it discourages flies. As it was the house tree there were taboos, and perhaps still are, against cutting it. We let it grow for its flowers and berries and although there is a whole lot more besides, these are arcane mysteries best left to the herbalist. I believe some of the by-products are dangerous. Of course, if the elderberry is so generally available locally that its flowers and berries can be got for free, it is not essential in the garden farm.

A bay tree and rosemary bushes must be cultivated to provide herbs which are difficult to buy fresh. Both shrubs are very pretty, particularly the little blue flowers of the rosemary. Both will provide many more herbs than needed by a family and the surplus can be sold at the garden farm gate or given to friends. Use both bay leaves and rosemary for cooking and rosemary in the bath or as a rinse after washing your hair.

A luxury to fill an odd corner is lemon verbena. Ours grows out of a crack in the house foundations. It is delicate, and except in the south needs protecting in the winter when it dies back to the stump. It grows strongly in the summer and its crushed leaves smell wonderful; they are useful in cooking because they impart fragrance and taste to milk puddings, and reduce the sugar requirement.

The hazel gives nuts, and a ready supply of pea boughs and bean sticks. These cannot really be got for free in the countryside as farmers and landowners quite reasonably will object to people hacking into hedges and woodlands.

A fig tree is easily grown against a south-facing wall, and nature's larder has few treasures to compare with a freshly picked fig. There is more to growing figs than you might think, and fresh-fig eaters are strongly recommended to read *Figs out of Doors* by Justin Brooke. Fig trees can also be grown orchard fashion like apple trees. Basic points to watch for are confining the roots, plenty of water in the May–June drought period and bagging or netting the nearly ripe figs to keep birds and wasps at bay.

The holly is an attractive tree to plant, and has a great show of berries all ready for the house and for friends. Male and female trees are needed for berries. We already have mistletoe so have never had to propagate it, but I'm told that if you rub a piece on to old apple trees you may get it started.

You do not have to have an orchard to grow apple trees, which show a good return if grown in tubs or odd corners. There are many quick fruiting apples available now which produce within two years of planting. As well as the fruit itself, there is cider and wine to be got, and geese and sheep feed on the windfalls.

In the long term, and it is impossible to be a true tree man without thinking long-term, every garden should have a walnut tree. I once lived in a caravan beneath a walnut tree and my memory of the nuts drove us once to holiday in France just so that we could cycle from village to village eating fresh walnuts. In the hot summer of 1976 our own village walnut tree cropped prodigiously.

Pretty trees to have, taking up small space and producing fruit which makes delicious jelly, are the rowan or mountain ash and the ornamental crabapple, a visual feast in flowering and fruiting. Wild crabs are unreliable fruiters and once we had made our first crabapple jelly we knew that our larder should never again be without it, and the only way to be sure of this was to grow our own. Rowan jelly goes well with game. Equally pretty and with delicious fruits are the medlar and quince trees. The medlar is eaten when rotten or made into jelly. The quince fruits like an apple and smells heavenly. Quince marmalade, purée, and ice cream are some of the delights to be made. Both trees are decorative and take up little room.

Planting vines is now the vogue after our series of hot summers. They can take up very little room – against a wall under a cloche – and the right sort can be planted against ugly walls and garages and allowed to romp away. We have only just planted ours, in corners rather than professionally in rows, and they all have started well except one. But the grower's notes say that it may take up to six months to emerge from dormancy, so we have not given up hope.

The vine that gives muscat grapes, my favourite, is in the best position looking south. There is one which will leap around a doorway if it grows according to plan, two which will grow modestly, producing grapes for wine, and one which will cover everything, producing 'small grapes' the children will love. Joanna's mother's ornamental grape fruited in its second year and I noticed that it attracted a lot of wasps, so they are better grown well away from open summer bedroom windows. We made wine with her grapes, three bottles in all. It tasted like a pleasant alcoholic grape juice. There are plenty of people now growing vines seriously, hoping for a good yield from quite small areas of ground.

Everything we read about grapes in England seems to have the vines growing on chalk – the viticultural centre at Limpsfield for example (now closed down after many years and incorporated with Jackmans of Woking) – but we garden on clay and we now think that vines will grow just about anywhere on anything provided their basic requirement can be met – plenty of sun and not much wind. The great English greenhouses of the past had wonderful grapes but we seem nowadays to rely on Belgian hot-houses for the best. We would like to have our own hothouse grapes but we decided against a vine in the greenhouse simply because we need the space for basics – tomatoes, cucumbers and such.

Trees either planted or growing wild can be harvested for local English versions of the great wines and fine Indian and China teas. A lime tree has a blossom whose heady scent will drench a whole garden, and bees carpet the grass under it, dying gloriously drunk by the thousand. Gathered and dried, the blossoms make tea. Elder blossom also makes tea, and both are medicinal. Vine prunings can be used likewise.

These British country wines and teas all have a distinctive taste quite unlike the real thing, and once we became accustomed to it we were hooked. A herbal tea is not tea. A country wine is not wine. Both are separate types of drink, in no way inferior to the Indian or French varieties, simply different. Hot elderberry wine on a cold winter day has a role in the household economy which no 'real' wine can fill. That is not to say, however, that country wines cannot be made deliberately to imitate the French wine. After all, elderberries were exported from Kent to France in the Middle Ages and, much more recently, rhubarb from Yorkshire for use in wine making.

Instructions for wine making will vary quite widely from book to book, and some are even contradictory. But if a method has worked for somebody else then it will presumably work again, although some of the nuances of temperature control and yeast growth are often inadequately explained.

Drying herbs seems much less of a business. The counsel of perfection tells how to dry at such and such a temperature to keep maximum nutritional, flavour and colour values, but herbs are so powerful and we need so little of them that perfection seems un-necessary. We just dry them until brittle in the low heat oven of our Aga, keeping the door open, or simply hang them up in bunches or a bit of old netting in an airy dry place. When brewing up we simply add enough to suit our own tastes, for no two teapots seem alike.

All in all, with food and drink for you and your animals, and fuel and aids in the garden, your garden trees will be an essential part of your garden farm, and as tree shepherds you may have found the basis of a garden farm fortune – and certainly a lot of pleasure.

CHAPTER ELEVEN

Health and the Home Farm

THE BENEFITS of farming your garden far outweigh the potential health hazards, many of which are extremely rare and can mostly be minimized almost to vanishing point by sensible precautions. Thus, I hope that the following catalogue of some rather alarming risks that may be run will not stop anybody working and keeping animals in the garden. Anybody who has a garden at all, even the most correct lawn-and-roses kind, or keeps a dog or a cat, is already at some risk, and you do not find gardeners deterred by the danger of tetanus or old-age pensioners bothered about their budgies.

The garden-farmer will find it impossible to avoid taking exercise and this in itself increases well-being, reduces the stress of crowded communal living and probably diminishes the chance of succumbing to the West's most common killer: atheroma, the cause of coronary thrombosis and strokes. If the healthy outdoor life enables the reader to give up smoking and forays to the kitchen for nibbles between meals, then these positive benefits will be further increased. The two groups of people who live longest in our society are, according to one survey, conductors of orchestras, and odd-job gardeners. These people have three things in common: they take plenty of exercise, they enjoy what they do and they never retire.

In a time of inflation many people economize on food and there have been various rather disquieting indications that health may be suffering as a result. The garden-farmer can afford the best because it comes from his own land and his own efforts; there will be no need for skimping on vegetables and fruit, or putting up with inferior meat. Such are the benefits. The hazards are infections from animals, physical strains, allergies and accidents.

ANIMALS AND HEALTH

Animals that are ill can pass certain diseases to human beings, the most important being brucellosis and T.B. Brucellosis can cause cows to abort and it can be passed to humans who handle infected cows or who drink untreated milk from a cow with brucellosis. Vets often catch the disease this way. In humans, brucellosis usually leads to periodic feverishness and it used to be known as undulant fever. The cure is a lengthy business and it can even prove impossible to get rid of the illness completely. When buying a cow, it is important to buy one from a herd which is certified free of the disease and to have her checked regularly by the vet. Raw milk from any dubious source should always be boiled. Should you have to handle a cow's tail end, wear surgical gloves and scrub your hands thoroughly afterwards.

T.B. is no longer the danger that it was, as it has been eradicated from milking herds in this country. However, there is always the very small risk that cows may be infected by tubercular wild animals, and there has been some anxiety about badgers particularly. Again, if in doubt boil the milk and in the case of your own cow ask the vet if he would advise a check.

Various skin rashes can also be passed to humans, the most famous example being cowpox, a mild infection of the hands caught from handling the infected udders of cows. William Jenner's observation that milkmaids who had previously developed cowpox could not catch the deadly smallpox led to the introduction of vaccination and has saved millions of lives.

Untreated milk

The risk of catching very serious diseases from raw milk has been discussed; stomach upsets and diarrhoea (gastro-enteritis) can also be caught from raw milk, particularly if it has not been kept in scrupulously clean containers, has been left in a warm place or has not been covered against flies. In small children especially such an infection can be serious and untreated milk should always be boiled for them; adults will probably feel, as we do, that the small risk is worth taking, for fresh, untreated milk is delicious.

Eggs

Eggs are perfectly wholesome and clean in themselves but if they are laid in polluted places they may become polluted through their shells; this is particularly so in the case of ducks' eggs, firstly as the shells are slightly porous, secondly because ducks will lay their eggs anywhere, even in the pond, while hens are tidier altogether and stick to their nice clean nesting boxes. There have been cases of gastro-enteritis poisoning from eggs, usually ducks' eggs, but if the eggs are thoroughly cooked there is no danger.

Meat

Animals killed at slaughterhouses have been carefully inspected for disease; home-killed meat of course will not have been inspected, so it should be cooked more thoroughly than meat from the butcher and whoever does the butchering should wash his hands carefully afterwards. These precautions should ensure that if, unnoticed by you, the animal was infected with disease when killed, there will be no danger to those eating the meat. Never eat meat from an ailing animal or one that has been on a course of drugs.

Raw meat could infect pets, so their meat should always be cooked, and particularly if it has been sold for use as pet food; home-killed meat should also be thoroughly cooked for pets, or they may themselves become a source of infection.

Infection from animal droppings

Many germs live in the gut, so should any animal have an infection, it might be passed to humans through its droppings. Wash thoroughly after mucking out any animals, and keep flies, which may have settled on the dung, out of the kitchen and the larder. The same applies to pets, particularly dogs, which have unpleasant habits in this respect; they should be kept out of the kitchen and given their own bowls. Droppings may also contain worms, or the larvae of worms. Some worms are not harmful to humans but two dog ones are highly dangerous. They can cause blindness, or fits. Dogs are far and away the most common source of worms, and they should be wormed in puppyhood and regularly thereafter. The touching sight of toddler and puppy sharing a plate is dangerous sentimentality and should be absolutely forbidden.

Tetanus, rabies and anthrax
These are very rare but often fatal infections that may worry the more widely read garden-farmer.

Tetanus is a paralysis that may occur if cuts become infected with soil that has been contaminated, even distantly in time, with horse or cow dung. It cannot occur in an individual who has been actively immunized against the disease. Active immunization with a course of three injections and booster every five years must be distinguished from the much less effective and very short-lived protection, passive immunization, which can be given after a cut has occurred. Any gardener who has not been actively immunized against tetanus is a fool. Incidentally, children who have received their routine jabs in recent years will have received such a course and only need occasional boosters.

Immunized or not, any garden cut should be encouraged to bleed freely and should be well washed with running water. If it is very deep, is contaminated with soil, or if there is any doubt about the degree of immunity you have against tetanus, medical advice should be obtained.

Rabies is a uniformly fatal brain inflammation that may develop up to nine months after the victim has been bitten by a dog, fox, or even bat infected with the virus. Fortunately, no infected animals exist in the U.K. so we need have no alarms at present, but officials are very worried that some criminal animal-lover, otherwise a model citizen, will break this happy state by thoughtless animal smuggling.

Anthrax is another infection from cuts or scratches contaminated with infected material of animal origin. Initially a rather unusual boil or eschar develops, followed in some cases by rapid spread of infection through the bloodstream. Death soon follows if antibiotics are not given. The main source of infected material used to be imported bonemeal but if this is sterilized, as it now is, there is no danger.

PHYSICAL STRAINS
Any healthy person under, say, forty benefits enormously from exercise, however unaccustomed, but after forty it is wise to start any new activity gently and work up to hard exercising if there is no medical reason for rest or restricted activity. The Royal College of Physicians has recently published a report stressing the benefits of exercise in middle age, provided that there is a gradual build up in muscular activity. When fit, one should exercise to

the point of breathlessness at least twice a week. I do not find that there are many jobs connected with the garden or the animals that make me breathless, but all that fresh air and well-being makes one more inclined to play a vigorous game of tennis or bicycle uphill as well as down.

The most common ailments connected with physical activity are backache and slipped discs. Human backs appear to be very badly designed for their job. However, the risks of hurting or straining the back can be very much reduced if two golden rules are always observed. Firstly, when lifting anything at all heavy, get as close to it as possible and have it directly in front of you, not out to the side. Secondly, always lift with your back kept ramrod straight and as vertical as possible; the effort should come from the legs, and the knees should do the moving. Like a tennis player, let your legs, not your body, do the work.

Allergies

Hay fever and allergies are much less of a bother now than they were. For many sufferers it is no longer necessary to rely on the anti-histamine drugs with their unpleasant side effect of sleepiness. Two types of nasal spray have become available which may prevent the onset of hay fever if used regularly over the pollen season. They are only available on a doctor's prescription, so those who find hay fever a nuisance should ask their doctor if the nasal sprays would be suitable in their case.

Accidents

Children are the people most at risk from accidents in the garden; it is a frightening thought that accidents are the most common cause of death in children, and half the total number of deaths occur at home. For children under five, road accidents are responsible for most deaths, followed by falls, fire and drowning, in that order. There have been well-publicized campaigns to reduce accidents in the home, but less attention has been given to risk in the garden. The danger of falls is obvious, but less well known is the frequent drowning of toddlers in garden pools or rainwater butts. Often it is the neighbour's grandchild who comes through the fence, or a visiting child, who is most likely to suffer. Fire can be a serious menace if hay or straw is stored where children may hide to practise striking matches. Older children may get into trouble with bonfires. Garden machinery should be kept locked away and it is better to get rid of young children before tackling jobs with dangerous machines. At no time is this more true than when a chain saw is being used. If children – even quite old children – want to help in the garden they should be given jobs which are well within their capabilities and they should be carefully supervised and shown how to use safely any tools or machines. This may mean they are less likely to experiment dangerously when your back is turned. Finally, there is the increasing danger from chemicals and poisons. Paraquat, paraffin, pesticides and many other deadly solutions should be kept *locked* away. They should never be decanted into drinks bottles, a habit that has often been responsible for tragic accidents.

Cuts and grazes can become infected, so they should be well washed in warm water, as described for the prevention of tetanus, before being covered with a plaster. Antiseptic ointments and lotions have only psychological value; they are not really worth using as they do as much harm to the body's defences against infection as they do to any germs which may be present!

If someone is unlucky enough to have such an injury as to cut his leg with an axe, or to have a head wound, very severe bleeding may occur. If it does, obviously you will immediately call the doctor but it is important to reduce the bleeding while waiting for him to arrive. Lay the injured person on the ground, make a pad out of a shirt or folded handkerchief and press firmly on the bleeding area.

Should you be unfortunate enough to remove an entire finger or toe, or even a limb, it is a good idea if it comes with you in the ambulance to hospital. It may be possible to re-attach it!

Animal bites should be treated with respect, as they can easily go nasty. Encourage bleeding by a good scrub under running water, and go to the doctor if the bite is a bad one or if it becomes red and swollen over the next few days.

Keep a wary eye on all animals: cows can kick, ponies can bite and kick, and pigs can knock you over (it is a bad idea to let children go into sties on their own).

Head injuries from kicks or falls may very occasionally lead to unconsciousness. The biggest worry if this does happen is difficulty with breathing, because the windpipe is obstructed.

The unconscious person should be laid on the ground on his side, any tie or collar should be loosened and should he have false teeth or a plate these should be removed and any vomit or other obstruction cleared from his throat. If he is still not breathing artificial respiration is the next resort. Pull his jaw firmly up and away from the neck, to straighten out his windpipe, and blow into his mouth enough to expand his chest (you will have to pinch his nose shut while blowing). Let his breath escape, then repeat the process about once every four seconds until help arrives or he starts to breathe naturally.

Anyone who has been knocked out, however briefly, should consult the doctor, as bleeding inside the head can occur up to several days later. Even after minor blows in the head, if the injured person feels unusually sleepy, or vomits or has a bad headache, a doctor should be consulted at once just in case there is a complication of this kind.

Stings and snakebites of the British variety are fortunately not a very serious danger. Bee stings should be removed, or they may go septic. Be careful not to squeeze the poison sac at the base of the sting. Adder bites almost always cause more fright than threat to life. If bitten by an adder, lie quietly while waiting to go to hospital and this will slow down the spread of the poison. Probably no treatment will be necessary, only observation, but anti-venom can be given if the bite is severe.

Sunburn can be very painful but is easily prevented by wearing enough clothes and using a barrier cream; lotions are fairly use-less but barrier cream protects by the thickness of the layer of application.

When working hard in hot weather, the body loses a great deal of salt as well as liquid through sweating, so have plenty to drink and add extra salt to food.

Sources of help

It is most unlikely that the garden-farmer will have health worries or need expert advice. If any animal or pets are ill consult the vet, who will tell you if there is anything wrong which could be communicated to people. If you or your family have mysterious symptoms, it would be sensible to tell your doctor what animals you are keeping, just in case there may be a connection.

General questions about public health matters can often be answered on the telephone by the area community physician, whose number can be found under the area health authority.

FURTHER READING

For those who wish to terrify themselves further, there is Donald Hunter's classic, *Diseases of Occupations* (E.U.P., 1969), a 1,200-page mine of erudition about farming as well as many other pursuits. Another fascinating book is Bisseru's *Diseases of Man Acquired From His Pets* (Heinemann, 1967). Despite the title, pets are predominantly taken to mean farm and domestic animals, but range from jackals to scorpions.

EXHIBIT A   EXHIBIT B

CHAPTER TWELVE

The Garden Farm and the Law

£8,500 FOR DAMAGE BY NEIGHBOUR'S TREES

A couple whose home started to crack up because of the growth of tree roots from a neighbouring garden were awarded £8,513 damages by a High Court judge yesterday.

A men's outfitter, Mr Ronald Conway, and his wife Jean, of 3, Heather Walk, Edgware, Middlesex, sued Mr Bedo Kalpakin, owner of No. 1, Heather Walk.

Mr Kalpakin denied liability. His counsel, Mr Alan Wilkie, said there was no way Mr Kalpakin could have known that the tree roots might cause damage to the Conways' home.

But Mr Justice Nield said it should have been clear that tree roots do cause damage to property. He also held Mr Kalpakin responsible for damage caused to Mr Conway's Citroen car when one of the trees was blown down in 1974.

The damages covered the cost of repairing the Conway's house, the damage to the car, and resulting invonvenience.

The Court was told the Conways found cracks and damage to their hall, kitchen, stairway, landing, bathroom and bedroom when they returned from a holiday in 1973. A trench revealed roots from next door pointing towards the house.

Daily Telegraph, January 1977

THE LAW, which affects every part of our lives – whenever we go out in a car, fill in our tax returns, lose the national census form, take a job or buy a pig – is a mystery to most of us. Information is difficult to obtain; law books are scarce in public libraries and appallingly expensive to buy. I am lucky to have a brother who is a barrister, and he has helped me with this chapter. Though it is no more than a brief summary of the law as it affects starting and running a garden farm, whether on a small or large scale, it may alert you to the cases where you might have a brush with the law or ought to take expert advice from a solicitor.

There are three main areas of the law which affect the garden-farmer. First, there are regulations and laws governing the way things are done – for example, requirements for planning permission to put up a shed, or for a licence to sell produce. Second, there is the law relating to nuisance, which neighbours can invoke if they object to what is going on in your garden. Third, there is the question of liability to other people, if they are injured or their property damaged as a result of garden-farming.

In most cases you are only liable to other people for injury or damage if you have failed to be reasonably careful, for it will have to be shown that you have been negligent. This is known as 'ordinary liability'. But in certain important exceptions you are automatically liable for damage or injury, no matter how careful you may have been. This is called 'strict liability'. In the following summary I have made it clear where strict liability may be involved because, obviously, in these cases one must be particularly aware of what one is about.

The law and animals

What would happen if your goat charged a friend of yours, bowled him over and broke his hip? Are you liable if a car, swerving to avoid your cow which had broken through on to the road, hits a telegraph pole? What would be your position if your sheep wriggles through the fence into your neighbour's garden and eats all his Brussels sprouts? You might find yourself in a tricky legal situation as well as an embarrassing one; following is a list of heads under which you might be in trouble.

1 Animals with an abnormal characteristic: strict liability

To start with a situation which, though by definition unlikely, could be extremely serious, you are *strictly liable* for injury to people or damage to property caused by an animal of yours having an 'abnormal characteristic'.

This liability only arises where the animal in question is unlike the majority of its species in that it has a tendency to be dangerous in a particular way and this tendency is known to you.

For example, Richard has a horse which, unlike most horses, bites people who come too close. This horse bites his friend Mary; as a result she loses the use of one finger of her left hand and has an ugly scar. Richard knew that his horse was apt to bite, so he is automatically liable to Mary and the only thing to be settled is the extent of the damages he will have to pay. This can be settled privately, probably with the help of solicitor's advice, or in court.

It might not be only Richard who is liable to Mary. If Richard were under sixteen, his father, or whoever is the head of his family, would also be liable. If the horse did not actually belong to Richard but was on loan from its owner, then its owner would also be liable.

All this applies wherever the accident may happen, whether the horse breaks through a hedge into a neighbour's land and bites the neighbour, or strays on to the road and bites the road-sweeper.

However, there are three cases where liability would not exist under this head:

(a) When the injured person voluntarily accepted the risk. In Richard's case, if he had warned Mary that the horse was likely to bite and she had gone ahead and stroked it in spite of this warning, then she would have voluntarily accepted the risk and Richard would not be strictly liable.

(b) When the injury was wholly the fault of the injured person. For example, if Mary had been savagely ill-treating the horse she would have only herself to blame if it bit her.

(c) When the injured person was trespassing. For example, if Mary had not known Richard and had come on to his land without asking permission. But this exception would never apply if the accident happened on the road, because then, of course, the injured person could not possibly be trespassing.

2 Taking animals on to the road: ordinary liability

When leading or driving animals along the road, you must keep them under control. Obviously, they must not be left unattended on the road. You could be liable if it can be shown that your negligence led to an accident or damage to property, so you must be able to show that you took every care that a reasonable person should. What is reasonable? This would depend on circumstances. One person can take a pony down the road, but you might need four men to drive a bunch of bullocks. Again, you might send your small daughter out to fetch the geese home along a tiny lane in a remote country area, but this would not do if you lived on a main road.

3   Animals which stray on to the road: ordinary liability

If animals stray in the road through the owner's negligence, the owner is liable for any damage or injury caused, so he must take every reasonable care to keep his animals off the road. This means that he must look after his fences and keep his animals provided with food and water so that they will not break out in desperation.

An animal that is really determined to break out will probably manage it. Cows have been seen to jump five-barred gates for what one can only presume are frivolous reasons, as there was no shortage of food, water or company. If the fence was in good repair and the animals well looked after, then the owner could show that he had taken every reasonable care to keep his animals off the road and he will therefore not be liable for any damage they may do. The busier the road concerned, the more care he must take.

Exception: there is no obligation to prevent your animals from straying on to the road if the land is common land or if the area is one where fencing is unusual, or if the animals are on a village green, provided that you have the right to graze them there.

4   Animals which stray on to other people's land: strict liability

The general rule is that it is up to the owner of animals to keep them from straying on to other people's land; you must fence against your own stock.

It is extremely important to maintain a good fence between you and your neighbours, because if your animals stray on to someone else's property you are strictly liable for any resulting damage or injury and will also have to repay him for the cost of detaining the animals.

However, this might not apply if:

(a) The animals went on to someone else's land from the road, while you were driving them along it, provided that you had taken every reasonable care to control them while they were on the road.

(b) It was wholly your neighbour's fault that the animals strayed on to his land. He might have broken down a perfectly good fence between the two properties, for example.

(c) The repair of the fence was not your responsibility, but the definite responsibility of someone else, who might be the neighbour in question or another person altogether. For example, if your neighbour had agreed under a binding contract to keep a fence in repair, had failed to do so, and as a result your sheep got through and broke his cucumber frame, you are not liable.

DISEASED ANIMALS

1 Liability
Another way in which animals can do harm is by becoming ill and passing the infection to other animals or even human beings. If this happens through the owner's carelessness he will be liable. So to avoid liability, you should take every care to prevent disease spreading. Isolate sickly animals, bury or burn carcasses and do not let other people touch them or other animals near them. If the disease seems serious or unusual or if more than one animal is affected, call the vet to find out what is wrong and what precautions should be taken. All this could be used in your defence, to show that you have not been negligent.

2 Statutory obligations
There are various 'notifiable diseases' which must be reported to the police if they occur.
The most important are:

cattle plague or rinderpest	sheep scab
contagious pleuromania of cattle	brucellosis
foot and mouth	swine fever
sheep pox	swine vesicular disease

There are also the less common notifiable diseases:

rabies	encephalomyelitis
anthrax	equine virus abortion
parasitic mange (in horses)	African horse sickness
tuberculosis	African swine fever
epizootic lymphangitis	Teschen disease
epizootic abortion	vesicular exanthema
infectious equine anaemia	dourine

So if you keep animals, that is 'cattle' (bulls, cows, oxen, heifers and calves), sheep or goats, any other ruminating animal, pigs, horses, asses, mules or jennets, and if one of the above diseases occurs, you have a statutory obligation:
1   to tell the police.
2   to keep the ill animal away from other unaffected animals.
   The Ministry of Agriculture, Fisheries and Food will deal with
L

the slaughter of infected animals and with the compensation for the owner.

POULTRY

Fowl pest in any form including Newcastle disease and fowl plague must be reported. The veterinary inspector must be informed in the case of Newcastle disease, and fowl plague must be reported to the police.

If you fail to report them, you can be fined up to £400 if more than ten animals are involved, or £50 for each animal, on a first conviction. If you are convicted a second time, you can go to prison for a month.

CRUELTY TO ANIMALS

Very few people would be deliberately cruel to animals but it is possible to be cruel through ignorance. Examples of cruelty which would probably be unintentional are: not giving an animal enough to eat (which can happen if you do not understand its food requirements, and I have described how it happened with two of our geese); causing a cow to suffer by not milking her; turning out a very lame horse to graze when you should have brought its food to its stable; failing to destroy an animal which is badly injured or ill. It is an offence to ill-treat an animal by cruelly beating, kicking, over-riding, over-loading, over-tiring, torturing, terrifying, or abandoning it. Should you have to operate on an animal, it is an offence to fail to operate as humanely as possible.

Cruelty to animals is punishable by a fine not exceeding £50 or by three months' imprisonment, or both. In addition, the magistrate can order that the animal should be taken away from the offender. If he offends again, on a subsequent conviction he can be disqualified from keeping animals of the kind in question, or from keeping any animals at all.

REGULATIONS FOR THE SLAUGHTER OF ANIMALS

There is nothing to stop anyone from slaughtering animals or poultry on his own property, provided that he is not going to sell the meat. The slaughtering must be carried out humanely. (See above under 'Cruelty to animals'.)

If it is intended to sell the meat, the animals must be slaughtered at a licensed abattoir. It is possible to ask the local authority for a licence to use your buildings as a 'slaughterhouse', but the authority will only give a licence if satisfied that the construction, equipment, cleanliness and so on are up to the required standards.

There are stringent regulations governing the sale of food and these are discussed at the end of this chapter (see pages 166–9).

NUISANCE

If your neighbours are bothered or annoyed by what is going on over the fence, or coming over or under it, they may be able to bring an action against you for nuisance. There are two main types of nuisance, one where there is an actual physical encroachment on a neighbour's land or property by such things as overhanging trees, and one where there is an undue interference with enjoyment of land or property by such intrusions as noise, smell or smoke.

Trees are the most common offenders where physical encroachment on to adjoining property is concerned. Their roots can spread over a considerable distance and their branches likewise. People are entitled to lop branches of neighbours' trees which overhang their land, without asking permission, so long as they do not go on to their neighbour's land to do this. Similarly, they can prune roots which grow through a boundary on to their land, without asking permission. They are not allowed to poison such roots, for this might damage the tree and if it does they are liable for the damage. They are not allowed to prune or lop roots or boughs which have not reached the boundary as a precautionary measure because they look as though they might soon encroach on their land.

Incidentally, the lopped boughs, with any fruit that may be on them, remain the property of the owner of the tree and should be returned to him. If they are not returned, he can sue for their value. Fruit that falls over a boundary also belongs to the owner of the tree and he has a right to go on to his neighbour's land to collect it, so long as he does no damage while he is there and takes no more time about it than he needs.

The roots of a tree can do considerable damage to buildings; an overhanging bough could fall and break a greenhouse; shade from overhanging branches could considerably reduce yield from an orchard or vegetable garden; a Virginia creeper could block gutters. If your trees or plants do this kind of harm to a neighbour's property he is entitled to damages and also to an injunction ordering you to remove the nuisance.

Nuisances which do not involve physical encroachment on other people's property are rather more difficult to pin down. Everyone has the right to use his land as he likes so long as he does not interfere excessively with his neighbours' enjoyment of their property; but an action can be brought against him to stop a nuisance if his behaviour could be held to be unreasonably objectionable. For example, he may have occasional bonfires to burn garden rubbish. His neighbour may hate the smell of bonfires, but there is nothing that he can do about it because reasonable people would agree that an occasional bonfire is justified. But if he burns piles of rubber tyres in his garden every evening, then this would be a nuisance. The crowing of cockerels might also be a nuisance, or the smell of a heap of pig manure, or the constant noise of a machine such as a chain saw. The trouble is that individual cases are often not clear-cut. Something that would constitute a nuisance in a suburban area would probably not be a nuisance in the depths of the country; something that happens very occasionally might not be a nuisance while something that happens frequently would. But what if it happens *fairly* frequently, or if the engine is only *rather* noisy? It is a question of what a reasonable person would find objectionable and it is a question of degree.

Weeds

It is infuriating to see weed seeds floating on to your garden from next door, but people are not liable to their neighbours for this. In the case of ragwort, and certain thistles and docks, the Ministry of Agriculture, Fisheries and Food may serve a notice on the occupier of the land to stop the weeds spreading, and he can be fined if he does nothing about it.

Sprays

Poisonous dusts or liquids can very easily drift on to adjoining property and if any harm is done to crops, fish, animals or land the neighbour can sue for damages. In extreme cases, where there is a threat to health or property, he can apply for an injunction to stop the spraying immediately and in an emergency this can be very quickly granted.

EMPLOYMENT

Any offers of help in the garden, paid or unpaid, are usually extremely welcome and accepted with joy, but here are some sobering facts.

Liability for injury to employees, family and friends

1 *Injury from defective equipment:* Usually an employer is liable to anybody who, while working for him, is injured by a defective machine or piece of equipment. This applies in the case of part-time or casual labour and even unpaid labour from friends or

family. So it is essential to check that all machinery and equipment is in good order and not in remotely dangerous condition before allowing anybody to use it.

Perhaps a machine might have a dangerous fault which is not visible from the outside, although this machine has been regularly and recently serviced. In this case the employer would probably not be liable, because he would have taken every reasonable care to see that the machine was safe.

It is also possible that an accident might occur with a machine which was dangerous solely through the fault of the employee. For example the employee might take off a safety guard and use the machine without it. In the case of a child, however, the employer would be expected to make sure that the machine was being used as it should be.

2 *The need to warn and supervise:* Even if the machines were perfectly safe the employer would be liable for damages from an accident if he had not taken the trouble to warn of the possible risks and dangers of the work. If need be, he must supervise the work in its early stages until he is quite satisfied that the employee can use the machine safely. He should be particularly careful if a child is involved, and the younger the child the more careful he should be, and there would come a stage when he should not allow a child to use a machine at all, even under supervision.

3 *Employer's obligation to insure:* If you carry on any sort of business, you are now obliged under the Employer's Liability (Compulsory Insurance) Act 1969 to insure against liability for bodily injury or disease sustained by employees (including part-time and casual employees).

If your garden is not a 'business' because all produce is for home consumption only, there is no obligation to insure. But if you have a stall on the roadside and employ people, you will have to insure.

There is no need to insure if the employer is the 'husband, wife, father, mother, grandfather, grandmother, stepfather, stepmother, son, daughter, grandson, granddaughter, stepson, stepdaughter, brother, sister, half brother or half sister' of the employee.

The Act contains detailed provisions about who you should insure with and for what amount, etc. You must therefore ask your solicitor's advice if you find that you are obliged to insure. Failure to insure is punishable by a fine of up to £200.

If you are employing people but you are not obliged to insure, either because you employ your family or because you are not running a business, you may still want to insure against liability for accidents and so on; where insurance is not obligatory, it would be rash to assume that it is not necessary or prudent.

PLANNING PERMISSION FOR GARDEN SHEDS

Animals, foodstuffs, machinery and tools and some growing plants all need a roof over them and the garden-farmer will probably want to put up a shelter, tool shed or greenhouse, or adapt and improve existing sheds or buildings.

If he wants to build a garage, or stables, or a loose box, or any shed more than ten feet high (twelve feet high if it has a ridged roof), planning permission will be necessary. If he simply wants to put up a garden shed or greenhouse the general rule is that he does not need planning permission (provided that the shed is not too high, of course). However, it would be most unwise to rely on the general rule, because there is a host of local laws and regulations which apply in various areas, and it might well be that planning permission is necessary before any kind of shed, however small, can be erected in some areas. If a building for which planning permission is necessary is erected without permission, the owner may be ordered to demolish it, so it could be a tiresome and expensive mistake.

THE SALE OF FOOD AND OTHER PRODUCE

If your garden farm is very successful there may be a surplus of food to sell. All over the countryside there are garden-gate stalls; probably there is quite a large sale of meat which goes on privately as people have their lambs, pigs or bullock slaughtered. (It is of course an offence to sell meat which has been slaughtered at home: see page 162, Regulations for the slaughter of animals.) Before embarking it is just as well to be aware first of what the criminal offences are in relation to the sale of food, second, of what the local regulations are, and third, of what your liability would be if any other person suffered as a result of buying your produce.

1   Criminal offences to do with the sale of food

If you sell food which is unfit for human consumption, or pass it to someone else for selling, this is a criminal offence for which you can be fined up to £100 or imprisoned for three months, or both. Meat from an animal which had been injected with drugs before it was killed, tainted meat, meat from a diseased animal, are all examples of food which is unfit for human consumption.

There are also regulations to ensure the cleanliness of the food whether it is sold from your home, or a stall, or a shop; if these regulations are ignored the penalties are similar to those for selling food unfit for human consumption. The regulations are:

(a) Food for sale must not be handled or sold in a place which is insanitary.

(b) Articles of equipment used must be clean.

(c) There are regulations concerning sanitation in rooms where the food or equipment is handled or cleaned (e.g. water must be laid on at the premises).

(d) Any stall must carry conspicuously the name and address of the stallholder.

2   Other regulations governing the sale of food

Local authorities have their own regulations to do with the handling, wrapping and delivery of food, so before setting up shop find out from the authority what the bye-laws are.

Local authorities also provide the licences to keep a stall or sell food which are necessary under local acts.

Sale of milk and milk products

There are special regulations to do with the sale of milk, butter and cheese, including goat's milk and goat's cheese. You might want to sell milk and milk products yourself, or you might want to sell milk to a dairy, or you might want to sell milk for consumption on the premises, if you are a bed-and-breakfast landlady or run a farm restaurant or if a thirsty hiker turns up at your door. Unless the milk is to be drunk on the premises (or the butter or cheese eaten there) you will have to apply to the local authority for registration as follows:

If you want to sell milk or milk products yourself, you will have to be registered by the local authority as a 'dairyman' and your premises registered as a 'dairy'.

If you want to sell milk from your cows to a dairy you will have to be registered by the local authority as a 'dairy farmer'.

Further, anyone who sells cow's milk must be registered under the Milk Marketing Scheme.

Sale of wool

You are not allowed to sell wool from your sheep unless you are registered under the British Wool Marketing Scheme.

This does not apply to anyone who keeps four sheep or less (a 'sheep' being taken to mean one aged over four months) at any one time, so it would probably not apply to most garden-farmers.

Sale of potatoes

You are not allowed to sell potatoes unless you are registered under the Potato Marketing Scheme.

This does not apply if your potato acreage is less than one acre. So here again most garden-farmers would not be affected.

Hops

There is a similar scheme for the marketing of hops, but it is so unlikely that the garden-farmer will find himself selling even one hop that I think we may ignore the problem.

THE CONSEQUENCES OF SELLING BAD OR INFECTED FOOD

It is vital that any food sold should be clean, fresh and free from all infection because if you end up in court the damages could be astronomical. It is a criminal offence to sell food which is unfit for human consumption (see page 166) but on top of that you can be liable to other people, if they care to sue, in two ways.

First, you would have to pay back to them the money that they had spent on your bad food.

Second, and this is where you could be in real trouble, you are absolutely liable to anyone who is injured as a result of eating your food – so theoretically you could sell home-made pâté which was consumed by three hundred and fifty guests at a wedding, and if they all had food poisoning or worse as a result you would be liable to them all. Colossal damages can be awarded to people who have been injured. It might well be worth taking out an insurance policy to cover yourself against such claims.

Anyone suing you for damages would have to prove that you had been negligent. So if you had no reason to think that the food was or might have been bad or infected you would not be liable. Perhaps you knew that the food was not fit for human consumption and you warned the buyer of this. For example, you have some beef which is tainted and a man buys it from you for dog food. You point out to him that the meat is not fresh, stress that it is only fit for pet food and sell it to him at a cut price advising him to cook it very thoroughly before feeding it to his dogs. If the buyer then uses it for steak tartare (which is not cooked at all) and he and his family suffer from food poisoning as a result, you would not be liable. But if that buyer was not capable of assessing the situation because he was perhaps subnormal or a child, or someone who barely understood English, then you would still be liable.

Another possible defence for you might be that the buyer had inspected the food and should have seen for himself that it was bad (again always assuming he was capable of this!). So if you have a pile of peaches on your garden-gate stall and a woman comes up and selects a dozen peaches for herself, she would not be able to come and ask for her money back if she found that they were rotten in patches. But if you have the fruit carefully stacked so that the rotten patches do not show and you push a dozen peaches into a bag without letting the customer see them, then you will be liable.

Consequences of giving away bad food

If someone suffers as a result of eating your bad food, you are still liable even if that food was given and not sold.

Sources of help

A garden-farmer with any legal worry should really consult a solicitor, but solicitors are expensive. The Citizens Advice Bureau can often help. Legal aid might be a possibility and the Citizens Advice Bureau could help with this also. Often it is the local authority which should be consulted. Where insurance is concerned it is a good thing to consult an expert; your bank would help, or an insurance broker.

APPENDIX

Addresses and Resources

APART FROM those organizations mentioned in the text so far, there are many others who will provide help, information and encouragement to those wishing to set up their own garden farm, or who offer specialist equipment for sale. The following list, though not of course exhaustive, may nevertheless help readers considering farming their gardens.

General

COUNTRY GENTLEMEN'S ASSOCIATION LTD.
Icknield Way West, Letchworth, Herts.
Delivers supplies of virtually everything you need to your door, at a discount price – but you must be a member.

SELF-SUFFICIENCY AND SMALLHOLDING SUPPLIES,
The Old Palace, Priory Road, Wells, Somerset BA5 1SY.
Has a wide range of equipment, a nice catalogue, and will send purchases by mail order.

Poultry

BRITISH WATERFOWL ASSOCIATION,
Bell House, 111–113 Lambeth Road, London SE1.
Useful if you keep ducks or geese, whether domestic or ornamental. Its magazine, *Waterfowl*, gives addresses of breeders all over the country and contains lots of useful articles. It also provides a *Yearbook and Buyers' Guide*.

Anyone interested in pure breeds of poultry should acquire *British Poultry Standards*, the major reference book in its field. It costs £6.80, plus 45p for postage and packing, but it is worth it, and can be ordered from:

TRADE AND EDUCATIONAL SALES,
Iliffe Books, Butterworth Group, Borough Green,
Nr. Sevenoaks, Kent.

There is no reference work for commercial hybrid breeds, but *Poultry World* publishes an issue on the subject each November.

Movable arks for free-range hens can be bought from:
LEWES ROAD SAWMILLS LTD.,
Scaynes Hill, Sussex;

HIDE OF HAILSHAM LTD.,
Croft Works, South Road, Hailsham, Sussex;

M. A. DRAYTON LTD.,
Laughton, Gainsborough, Lincs.;

PARK LINES & CO.,
Park House, 501 Green Lanes, London N13 4BS.

A lot of money can be saved by having home-made arks, for the simplest ark costs around £50 new, and most are about £70. Second-hand arks are occasionally available at farm sales or through advertisements in local newspapers.

THE RELIABLE THERMOSTAT CO. LTD.,
95 Main Street, Bramley, Rotherham, Yorks.
This company supplies a 'Vision' 25-egg incubator for around £50, including carriage, packing and V.A.T., and instructions for use. There are also 50-egg and 100-egg incubators. The 'Vision' can be converted into a brooder once the eggs are hatched. Similar in price is the Sydenham Hannaford 'Ironclad' incubator, available from:
GILBERTSON & PAGE LTD.,
Corry's, Roestock Lane, Colney Heath, Herts AL4 0QW.

Albert drinkers and other poultry equipment are available from:
GEORGE H. ELT LTD.,
Eltex Works, Worcester WR2 5DW.

Goats

THE BRITISH GOAT SOCIETY,
Rougham, Bury St Edmunds, Suffolk IP30 9LJ.
Will send you a list of their available leaflets. This is extensive and covers all aspects of goat-keeping, including plans for a simple goat-house. They will also put you in touch with goat-keepers in your area.

JAMES HUNTER LTD.,
Farm Seed Growers and Specialists, Chester.
Will send you their farm seed catalogue. This gives special mixtures for hays, kales, lucerne and sainfoin, all worth sowing if

you have land and time. They also produce an interesting publication called *Hunter's Guide to Grasses, Clovers and Weeds*.

Comfrey plants may be obtainable from:
H.D.R.A., 20 Convent Lane, Bocking, Braintree, Essex.

Fred Ritson will send you his marvellous catalogue and plenty of free advice if you have a query. He supplies everything from milking pails to running tethers and is the only supplier of this kind in the country. His address is:
FRED RITSON,
Goat Appliance Works, Longtown, Carlisle, Cumbria.

Bees
THE MINISTRY OF AGRICULTURE, FISHERIES AND FOOD
Have some excellent bulletins on beekeeping, obtainable from H.M.S.O.: *Beekeeping* (Bulletin 9), *Beehives* (Bulletin 144), *Advice to Intending Beekeepers* (Advisory leaflet 283) and *Feeding Bees* (Advisory leaflet 412). H.M.S.O. publications cannot be bought through ordinary bookshops. Their retail bookshop in London is at:
49 High Holborn, London WC1V 6HP,
and also Manchester, Birmingham, Cardiff, Bristol and Belfast. Addresses in appropriate telephone directories under Her Majesty's Stationery Office.
The leaflets are also available from:
THE MINISTRY OF AGRICULTURE, FISHERIES AND FOOD
(PUBLICATIONS),
Tolcarne Drive, Pinner, Middlesex.
The British Beekeepers' Association can provide specifications for home-made hives (for these *utter accuracy* is essential, so unless you are a good craftsman, you should not make the attempt).
BRITISH BEEKEEPERS' ASSOCIATION,
General Secretary, 55 Chipstead Lane, Sevenoaks,
Kent TN13 2AJ.

For the B.B.K.A.'s magazine, *Bee Craft*, write to:
BEE CRAFT LTD.,
The Secretary, 21 West Way, Copthorne, Sussex.

Index